Anxious Church Anxious People

How to Lead Change in an Age of Anxiety

Anxious Church Anxious People

How to Lead Change in an Age of Anxiety

JACK SHITAMA

Charis Works

Published by Charis Works, Inc. in Earleville, Maryland.
Inquiries may be sent to info@christian-leaders.com.
Book cover and interior designed by Claire Purnell Graphic Design
Edited by Kendall Davis
Author photograph by Erin Shitama

ISBN 978-1-7320093-0-1 (Ebook)
ISBN 978-1-7320093-1-8 (Paperback)
ISBN 978-1-7320093-2-5 (Hardcover)
ISBN 978-1-7320093-3-2 (Audiobook)

Table of Contents

Introduction

If you are a church leader, clergy or lay, this book is for you. If you have a vision for the local church but can't get it done, look no further than this book. If you have tried various initiatives only to be met with resistance and anxiety, then you will recognize the examples that I offer. If you lead a congregation that has experienced a decades-long decline, then you know that their anxiety is focused on dwindling attendance, financial resources and relevance.

What I share is based on Edwin Friedman's seminal book, *Generation to Generation: Family Process in Church and Synagogue*. I first encountered it in 1991 while in seminary. It immediately changed my approach as a leader. It has enabled me to lead change in a variety of settings over the last 26 years.

I started teaching this to other leaders in 2002. I found that people had a hard time understanding the main concepts. People said when they tried to read *Generation to Generation* that it was "dense." It is. The concepts are deep. They apply to families, churches and organizations, but how they work is not easily grasped. I wrote this book to make Friedman's approach to leadership more accessible and practical. I explain the concepts in ways that people without a psychology degree can understand, by using examples to help you think about how the principles work in the real world.

When you complete this book, you will understand the process that keeps churches anxious and stuck, how leadership through self-differentiation gets churches unstuck and how you can develop as one who can lead through self- differentiation.

We start off with an examination of the "age of anxiety." Then I lay out the core concepts that will persist throughout this book about leadership through self-differentiation and the characteristics of an anxious church. This provides the context to teach you how to recognize and deal with the kind of anxiety that makes effective, lasting change nearly impossible.

The good news is that leading change, even in an anxious church, IS possible. The key is learning how to manage your own anxiety. This is not a quick fix. My own experience is that it is a life's work. But it is worth the effort. If you are up for it, you are likely to find that you will not only become a person who can lead change, you will be a better family member and better able to cope with stress. Not a bad deal.

If you're willing to make that journey, then let's get started.

You can access a FREE Companion Course to go deeper into the material presented in this book at: www.christian-leaders.com/anxious-book-course.

Chapter 1
An Age of Anxiety

An Anxious Society

The key to leading change is the ability to be a non-anxious presence. This is even more important in the church, where tradition and change are often at odds. This is especially true in an age of anxiety.

I don't mean anxiety in the clinical sense. I mean the inability to deal with uncertainty and the desire to control inputs and outcomes that is driven by a fear of failure. In Matthew 6, Jesus says, "Do not worry." The Greek word for "worry" in the text is best translated as "anxiety." And Jesus equates anxiety as a sign of little faith. The most troubling thing that I see in churches is Christians who say they trust in God, yet who fear the future. Rather than acting as the leaven of hope in an anxious culture, we Christians have allowed the age of anxiety to overtake the church.

I have been a camp director for 18 years. Since the terrorist attacks on September 11, 2001, I have seen parents and grandparents become more anxious about sending their kids to overnight camp. We don't allow cell phones, and the kids don't have time to call home. So, for six days and five nights, parents have to trust us to care for their kids. This is hard to do for many parents who are used to constant communication with their kids. We've had parents tell us they would keep their teenage children home from camp unless we changed our "no cell phone" policy, and others have even contacted us to make sure we were aware of the weather in the area. Even though their children were being cared for, it was too hard for many parents to let go of that control.

In *A Failure of Nerve: Leadership in the Age of the Quick Fix*, Edwin Friedman contends there are two indicators of what he calls a chronically anxious society: we choose safety over adventure, and we blame others for our problems.

We Choose Safety over Adventure

Safety, of course, is not a bad thing. We've had some great advances in the last several decades. Seat belt use, anti-lock brakes and air bags have made car travel significantly safer. Helmet use has reduced injuries from bicycling, skateboarding, skiing and water skiing. Computerization has made the commercial airplane one of the safest forms of travel. The age-adjusted death rate in America dropped 15.98% in the first decade of this century, mainly due to public health prevention efforts like vaccinations, auto safety, tobacco education, disease prevention and maternal/infant health improvement. Safety is a good thing, but it's important to not let the desire for safety morph into being overly fearful.

We have become a society that is afraid of everything. How does this affect leaders? We end up with leaders who want to play it safe. We have created a society where we punish those who take risks. Our anxiety and our desire for safety make us afraid to fail and afraid of the consequences should we take a leap of faith. Seth Godin once wrote that anxiety is experiencing failure in advance.[1] When we are a people who are constantly experiencing failure before it happens, we seldom take the kinds of risks that will move us forward or find solutions to our biggest problems.

We Blame Others for Our Problems

In an age of anxiety, we not only seek safety over adventure, but we also have a hard time taking responsibility for our situation. Rather than choosing how we will respond to the challenges in life, we blame others. Here are some examples. I will try to make everybody angry.

- We blame China or Mexico, or the American companies that move factories overseas, for our country's economic problems

- We blame terrorists for making us feel unsafe

- We blame the police for making us feel unsafe

- We blame the proliferation of guns for making us feel unsafe

- We blame government intrusion on the ability to arm ourselves for making us feel unsafe

- We blame big government for intruding in our lives

- We blame the lack of government intervention for keeping us economically oppressed

- We blame our elected officials for not getting anything done

- We blame the school system when our kids don't learn

- We blame parents when our students don't learn

- We blame liberals for promoting moral decay

- We blame conservatives for sustaining a white-dominated culture

Need I go on?

We are living in a country of victims where people are looking for someone to blame for their situation. I realize not

everybody is this way, but the political rhetoric today reso-
nates more with those who feel victimized than with people
willing to take responsibility for their own condition.

What can we do about this? We can take responsibility
for our own position by working toward self-differentiation. Self-differentiation is central to the family systems
approach to leadership, as explained in Edwin Friedman's
book *Generation to Generation*. It is defined as taking responsibility for one's own goals and values amidst surrounding togetherness pressures.[2] We'll unpack this in greater
detail throughout this book, as well as how best to apply it
to church leadership. For now, it's important to understand
that family systems theory teaches that the most significant
factor in how someone fares under hostile conditions is
their own response. Self-differentiation is the key to that
response. This book will not only help you to understand
what self-differentiation is, but it will also teach you how to
apply it in your family, church or organization. It will help
you to be an effective leader.

These days can feel like the conditions are hostile, trying to
raise a family or making an organization or church thrive.
A job loss is a hostile condition. Racism and sexism are
hostile conditions. Discrimination of any kind is a hostile
condition. We may have no control over many of the causes or manifestations of these conditions, but we can control
how we respond -- blaming is a manifestation of anxiety.
Instead of taking responsibility for ourselves, we blame others. When we do that, we've made it nearly impossible for
us to change our situation for the better. However, when
we take responsibility for our own condition, we have a
chance.

My father was born in Seattle, Washington, in 1921. He
was 21 years old when President Roosevelt signed Executive
Order 9066, which authorized the Secretary of War to de-
clare certain areas of the west coast of the United States as

military zones. That order enabled the relocation of about 120,000 persons of Japanese ancestry to internment camps in the interior west. Over 70,000 of the evacuees were American citizens, including my father and his four sisters.

My father and his family ended up at Minidoka Concentration Camp near Twin Falls, Idaho. He and other young men were sent out to surrounding potato farms to work on the harvest at below market labor rates. He managed an all-Nisei (second generation Japanese-American), 17-piece swing band. On weekends they would play at weddings and high school dances, where people hurled racial epithets, but enjoyed dancing to the music.

When the potato harvest ended and everyone went back to Minidoka, my father went to Salt Lake City. It's a bit of a mystery as to how this happened, but, needless to say, security was not great, because nobody came after him.

He found a New Deal program where he learned to weld. A man advised him to go east, where he would be safe from further internment. He went to Chicago and got a job with the Pullman Car Company, which was manufacturing tanks as part of the war effort. He was fired when it was discovered that he was Japanese-American.

Here's the point. My father had every right to blame FDR, and America in general, for his condition. He had nothing to do with Pearl Harbor and certainly did not deserve to be taken from his home to a camp in Idaho. But blame would have done him no good. It would make him a victim, but it would not fundamentally change his condition. Instead, he did what he could to survive. It did not involve seeking safety. It required adventure, risk and a willingness to fail. But, in his mind, this was far better than accepting things the way they were. When he had the opportunity to enlist in the U.S. Army, he did. He saw it as a way to prove his loyalty as an American, as well as a way to improve his life.

He used to tell us a story about his trip to Camp Bland-ing, Florida, for basic training. The bus he was on stopped somewhere in the Deep South. When he went to the rest-room he encountered two signs: "White" and "Colored." He went toward the colored bathroom.

A white man stopped him and asked, "Where are you going?"

He replied, "To the bathroom."

The man said, "You're not colored, you're white."

Everything he had experienced in the last several years told him he was not white. But this was the Jim Crow South, and the rules were different. My father used to finish this story by saying, "No matter how bad we had it, we never had it as bad as black people."

Which leads me to a more familiar example of taking re-sponsibility for one's own condition, as well as being a self-differentiated leader: Dr. Martin Luther King Jr. He did not focus his attention on blaming white people. He cer-tainly called out racism for what it was, but his message was one of love and hope. He led by sharing what he believed and asked others to join in. That is, he self-defined. He did not condemn his oppressors, but he showed the willingness to stay engaged through peaceful means.

Here are some of his self-defining statements:[3]

> "I have a dream that my four little children will one day live in a nation where they will not be judged by the color of their skin but by the content of their character."
>
> "I have decided to stick to love...Hate is too great a burden to bear."
>
> "As my sufferings mounted I soon realized that there were two ways in which I could respond to my situation -- either to react with bitterness or seek to transform the suffering into a creative force. I decided to follow the latter course."

Note the tone of Dr. King's statements. Non-anxious, but passionate. Pointed, but not blaming. He was anything but a victim.

Back to the focus of this chapter. We live in an age of anxiety. Who will seek adventure over safety? Who is willing to take responsibility for themselves, instead of playing the victim? I believe the future of the church depends on people who can do this. It depends on people who can be self-differentiated in an anxious society and an anxious church.

Chapter 2
Leadership through Self-Differentiation

Self-differentiation is the key to leadership in any family, church or organization, especially one that is chronically anxious. Friedman calls this leadership through self-differentiation:

"The basic concept of leadership through self-differentiation is this. If a leader will take primary responsibility for his or her own goals and self, while staying in touch with the rest of the organism, there is more than a reasonable chance that the body will follow. There may be initial resistance but, if the leader can stay in touch with the resisters, the body will usually go along."[1]

Leadership through self-differentiation is not about convincing others to agree with you. It is about who you are and what you believe. It is spending enough time in prayer and discernment to have a sense for where God wants you to lead. It's not even about being right; it's about what is best for the system, whether it's your family, your church, company or organization. And what's best for the system is for you to know who you are, what you believe and to express this in healthy ways. That's leadership. From this point forward, unless I note otherwise, when I say leadership, I mean leadership through self-differentiation.

There are two components to leadership: self-definition and emotional connection.

Vision is a big part of self-definition, as I'll cover in Chapter 5. However, self-definition is not just about the big picture. As a leader, it involves everything you do. Self-defining in a healthy way helps to reduce the overall anxiety in a system in a way that encourages others to self-define. As we'll see later in this chapter, in anxious systems self-defining will make things worse before they get better.

Self-defining is important because, as a leader, people look to you for direction. This is not just vision -- it's about every decision, every matter of substance. People want to know what you think. Perhaps an example will help.

Christmas will fall on a Sunday 14 times in the 21st century. The intervals between these occurrences are five, six or 11 years. Every time this happens, it raises the issue in many churches as to how to handle it. It's rather ironic, since it is Jesus' birthday, so going to church would make sense. Unless, of course, we acknowledge that Christmas is mostly a secular holiday, even for Christians. So imagine a conversation at a Worship Committee meeting. Whether you are the pastor, chairperson or member, you are a leader in the congregation. Leadership requires that you self-define. Here are some examples:

> "I believe it's important to honor the sacred nature of the day and stick with our two regular services."

> "I don't think it makes sense to have two services when attendance will be low in both. I think we should go with a combined service."

> "I think we should cancel church altogether and let people spend time with their families. I feel that the Christmas Eve service is where we celebrate Christmas anyway."

Who's correct? That is a matter of opinion. And opinions matter. But, from a family systems perspective, the objective is not to determine who is right and who is wrong. It is to express what you believe, while giving others the freedom to express their own beliefs. To do this, one must maintain emotional connection. Friedman calls this "staying in touch."

Self-defining without emotional connection is not leadership; it is narcissism. If you just say what you believe but cut yourself off emotionally from the rest of the group, they will stop sharing their opinions. If you've ever worked for a leader like this, you understand. People fear speaking up. They will usually wait for the leader to express her opinion, then chime in with agreement. This is especially true in corporate situations where the leader also has power over the followers' employment status. In any system, a narcissistic leader will not promote self-definition among others, but will stifle it.

Emotional connection values others as persons, even if they disagree (or are disagreeable). It is showing care and concern for the other, apart from the issue at hand. It is NOT kowtowing to the will of others. It IS respecting that the other is a SELF and honoring that self, without letting them define you. I find it helpful to think of emotional connection in terms of pastoral care. This is not just the work of the pastor. As Christians, we are all called to care for others. Healthy emotional connection is caring without overfunctioning. It's connecting to others with care and concern without being defined by them.

A wise pastor once told me, "People don't care how much you know, until they know how much you care." Leadership combines self-definition with genuine care. They can be seen as two separate functions because one is focused on a common mission and the other focuses on the individual. They can be seen as related because you can't be effective with just one.

The Non-Anxious Presence

An effective leader is a non-anxious presence.

A non-anxious, non-presence is someone who is not anxious, but is also not emotionally connected, not emotionally present. It's easy to be non-anxious when you don't care or don't have an emotional stake. A non-anxious, non-presence can be someone who is narcissistic. They self-define, but they couldn't care less about others. Or they can be highly adaptive in the negative sense. They can't self-define, so they just go along with others to protect themselves from having to self-define.

An anxious presence is someone who can't help but let their anxiety spew into the system. They care too much. They are so emotionally connected that they overfunction anxiously in others' emotional space. They react in anxious ways when others self-define. It can be with anger, blaming or passive aggressive behavior, but they will find an outlet for their anxiety and it won't be healthy.

It's important to point out that most of us don't function naturally in well-differentiated ways. Murray Bowen, the pioneer in family systems theory, said that self-differentiation is on a continuum with 0% being the worst and 100% showing complete differentiation of self. Bowen believed most of us function on the poorly differentiated end of scale. He, along with Friedman, believed we can improve our ability to become more self-differentiated. In family systems theory, this is called doing your own work. It is about understanding the emotional processes in your own family of origin. It is about reworking the family relationships that are your greatest sources of anxiety. We'll cover this more fully in Chapter 4. But even if you do your own work, Bowen believed 70% to be the upper limit for most people. This means that even the most emotionally healthy among us are only behaving in self-differentiated ways about 70% of the time.

Most people tend to function more toward one direction or the other. Some can be pretty easygoing, but tend to avoid having to self-define. Others are anxious people because they care so much. In either case, they are functioning on the lower end of the differentiation continuum.

There are two important points to understanding a non-anxious presence. The first is that being a non-anxious presence doesn't mean you don't feel anxiety. A non-anxious presence means you contain your own anxiety while staying emotionally connected. It is recognizing the anxiety and then being intentional to express yourself in a non-anxious way. This is called self-regulation, which I will explain more fully in Chapter 8.

This leads to the second point. The higher the emotional stakes, the more anxiety you are likely to feel. If there is nothing emotionally at stake, it's easy to be non-anxious. So when an acquaintance at work tells you she has a serious illness, you can show care and concern and not be anxious. When it's your parent or child, it's a lot harder. I've found the emotional stakes to be highest for me in my own family. This is true for most people. Next is the ministry I lead. Any place you are a leader, you will have higher emotional stakes than where you are not. Third is my church. I attend a church where I used to be the pastor. I was invited back after we had been gone for a few years. I'm very careful not to interfere with the pastor and, as such, do not have a great amount of involvement in the church, outside of playing in the band. Church often ranks second for Christians for a number of reasons -- the church is where they work out their own salvation, they may be functioning as a leader and the church is a family system made up of family systems. This last point helps to understand why people so often displace anxiety from their own family of origin into the family system that is the church.

Here is an example of high emotional stakes:

My mother was born in Seattle, but lived in Hiroshima, Japan, from age 10 to 24, which included World War II. Though my older brother and sister had been to Japan, I had not. My mother decided she wanted to take her three children and their spouses on a personal pilgrimage. This would not only be my first visit to my country of heritage, it would be my first with my family. And, with my mom at age 93 and my father having passed away three years prior, it was now or never.

As it turned out, my daughter and her boyfriend happened to be doing some extended travel and their first leg went right through Japan at the same time as our visit. I asked her if she could join us for at least part of the time. She emailed me to let me know that she had changed their itinerary to include a one-week stopover in Japan so they could join us for a good part of our trip. I felt a bit of anxiety about this, because I realized I had not checked with my mom or my siblings.

One side note: When we were planning the trip, my brother invited my mom's two sisters, ages 91 and 89, respectively, to join us on our trip. One of the sisters called a few weeks later to say they'd love to join us. After the phone call, my mom said, "I don't want them to come with us. I just want to go with my children." Very self-defined.

Then she tried to triangle me. The definition of a triangle is that when two people get uncomfortable in their relationship, the focus is on the third (see the next chapter on triangles). In this case, my mom was uncomfortable with her sisters, so she focused on me. If I would have taken the bait, then all the discussion that should have taken place directly between my mom and her sisters would have gone through me. This not only would allow my mom to avoid having to deal with her sister, but I would end up feeling the stress of the situation. Here's how the conversation went between my mom and me.

"Call my sisters and tell them I don't want them to come."

"I'm not calling them. They're your sisters."

"Then call your brother and tell him to uninvite my sisters."

"I'm not calling him. I'm fine with your sisters coming."

To her credit, my mom called her sister and extended the "uninvitation." They were fine with it.

Back to the trip.

My first challenge was to ask my mother if having my daughter along for part of the trip was OK. She said it was fine. When I reminded her that she had uninvited her sisters, she replied, "This is different. She's my granddaughter." Difference is in the eye of the beholder.

My next challenge was to check with my siblings. I emailed them to ask. My brother, the oldest, wrote back to say he was a little tossed up, but he would go with whatever mom wanted. My sister, the middle child, wrote back to say she, too, had mixed feelings. She noted that she loved my daughter and had recently spent some time with her when she was visiting the area where my daughter lives. But she had thought of the trip as being just my mom and her kids. She also didn't want the other grandchildren to feel left out. She asked if a few days would be reasonable compromise. I should point out that both of my siblings wrote using "I" statements, taking ownership of their own feelings. My own anxiety increased a notch.

Second side note: This email exchange took place while I was leading a retreat for church leaders with a heavy emphasis on family systems and leadership through self-differentiation. What kind of hypocrite would I be if I didn't handle this as a non-anxious presence? How could I self-de-

fine, yet stay connected? What should I do? Which emphasizes the points I am making. You WILL feel anxiety, and
the higher the emotional stakes, the more anxiety you will
feel. This is what surrounding togetherness pressures feel
like. Even though my siblings self-defined, I was feeling the
pressure internally. It was my problem, not theirs.

I did my best to self-define in this situation, but I also
thought that what my siblings were thinking was not unreasonable. Being self-defined doesn't mean you don't listen. It
just means you know what you want, believe, feel, and you
are able to own it. So I chose to go with a compromise.
My daughter would join us for three nights instead of six. I
called my brother and we talked. He was OK. I emailed my
sister knowing that she was out of pocket for a week and my
daughter needed to solidify her plans. My sister eventually
emailed back, saying she was fine with whatever we decided. She wrote, "Inclusion is best. Exclusion is not." As I re-
flected on this, I was proud of my family. We are not perfect.
But we were able to handle this as non-anxious presences,
controlling whatever anxiety we may feel, but expressing
our feelings and staying connected.

Being a non-anxious presence is intentional. It requires
being reflective enough that when you feel anxiety, you understand where it's coming from. This requires doing your
own work.

Doing Your Own Work

If you want to become better differentiated, you must do
your own work. There is no other way. This means you
need to dig into your family of origin. Your family of origin is comprised of your nuclear and extended family. It's
not just parents and siblings, but also grandparents, aunts,
uncles and cousins. If you can go back another generation
or more, that's better. The further back you go, the more
you will discover. Every family has its own set of unwritten

rules about how to do life. Whether it's raising children, handling money, dealing with conflict, spirituality, handling crises, ad infinitum -- there are certain ways to do it. It is like software or code that dictates how you respond to any given situation. And, absent of reflection or intentionality, you will react to each situation in the way that you are programmed.

A good example is how families handle holidays such as Christmas and Thanksgiving. Some families treat them as sacred, and everybody must be together. Others treat them as important, and everyone tries to get together, but if everyone's not there, it's no big deal. Some families don't even celebrate them. Some holidays are more important than others. In my wife's family, Christmas is a pretty big deal. Christmas is important in my family, but New Year's Day is my dad's birthday. So when he was alive, we most often spent Christmas with my in-laws and New Year's with my family.

The primary means for doing your own work is the genogram. A genogram is a family tree that also includes markings to illuminate the emotional dynamics present in the system. The final chapter of this book will describe how the genogram is used, along with other tools and resources, to help you understand how your family of origin influences your emotional functioning.

Doing your own work is especially important if you have a spouse. The software with which we have been programmed by our family of origin explains why couples have conflict. There are two different codes, and they aren't always compatible. A couple's life together depends on being able to recognize the software differences AND being able to work through them. The differences are most intense around money and raising children. But they crop up everywhere, down to whether the toilet paper hangs over or under the roll (the correct way is over, Google it). This doesn't mean they have to choose one system's software over the other. In any given circumstance they can choose one, the other or another way altogether. The most important thing is that they recognize the differences and are intentional about what they decide, even in the midst of surrounding togetherness pressures.

The process of recognizing differences and working through them forces an awareness of your family's software. It also develops an ability to take an emotional stand with someone close to you who is not a part of your family of origin. This is a key to leadership through self-differentiation. To the extent you have difficulty doing this with a spouse, you will have difficulty doing this as a leader. It's also a clue that you have unresolved issues that have their roots in your own family.

Doing your own work means looking at your family of origin to crack the code. It's not just understanding the software, but also understanding from where it comes. Who were the dominant personalities? Where was the dysfunction? What patterns repeat from generation to generation? Do any skip a generation?

Why does this matter? It matters because your ability to function as a non-anxious presence everywhere is rooted in your own functioning in your family of origin. To the extent that you have difficulty self-differentiating, it comes from difficulty doing so in your family of origin. It's how you are programmed. This is not to blame anyone in the system. It's a reality. When you start to unpack it, you gain awareness of how you are programmed. Once you have the awareness, you can begin to rewrite the code.

When you are in an anxiety producing situation, a good question to ask is, "Where does this come from?" That is, where did you experience similar anxiety in your family of origin? What was the nature of the relationship? How can you rework that relationship? The key understanding is that it is the residue from unworked out relationships that affect your ability to function as a non-anxious presence. An inability to self-differentiate in one or more relationships in your family of origin means that you have not worked it out. You have unresolved issues. You are likely to carry this into the other systems in which you function, making it harder to be a non-anxious presence. My own story illustrates this.

During childhood and as a young adult, I was rarely able to take an emotional stand with my mother. She was not dominating or cruel or even anxious. She was a strong personality. Whenever she said something, I complied. I had a normal enough childhood, so I didn't even recognize my adaptive behavior. How did this code work in my life? I was a conflict avoider. I did not know how to take an emotional stand, so I would stuff my emotions. Mostly, I learned to handle this, but every once in a while I would erupt like a volcano. As I looked back, I was just like my dad.

When I was 28, I heard the call to pastoral ministry. I did not grow up going to church, so I knew this would be hard for my mom to understand. But I also felt great conviction and peace about this. This gave me the resolve to tell her in a non-anxious way. After I called her, she responded with a steady stream of phone calls and letters where she kept asking me if I was sure about the decision. She mainly asked me about what I believed and whether I had considered the financial implications of the pastoral life. She didn't tell me I shouldn't do it, but it felt like intense surrounding togetherness pressure to me. Normally, I would have folded like a cheap lawn chair. But this was different. I felt compelled by God to move in this direction. My mom is a strong woman, but she's no match for God. So I was able to stay calm and firm. "Yes, this is what I feel called to do." I took an emotional stand. After a month, she called me to say that if I was sure about this, she and my dad would support my decision.

At the time, I wasn't actually doing my own work. It was a couple years later in seminary, when I first encountered family systems theory, that I started to realize that this was a turning point in my own emotional functioning. I was gaining a greater capacity to speak up for myself in a non-anxious way. The way I had functioned in the past was not my mom's fault. It was how I functioned in my own family of origin, especially in relation to my mother, and how I learned to respond. But by reworking how I was able to respond to my mom, I was better able to self-define in other situations in life.

Doing your own work, reworking relationships, is not about the others in your family of origin. It's about you. So you don't necessarily need another to be alive to rework the relationship. I know of one woman who realized that she had a lot of unresolved anger toward her deceased father. She wrote him a letter, then sat face to face with another person and role-played the interaction. She read the letter, imagining the other to be her father. The effect was clearly not on her father; it was on herself. Doing your own work is about what's inside of you. It's taking responsibility for who you are and how you function. It recognizes that there are other relationships that need reworking, but it doesn't blame the other.

How can you do this? For many, the most effective means is to see a counselor who has a background in the family systems approach and can help you do your own work. If that's not your thing, start by reading *Generation to Generation*. It's not an easy read, but it will help you dig deep into the details of how systems work, so you can better understand your family of origin and your own functioning in it. In either of these approaches, an essential element will be doing your own genogram. A genogram is like a family tree, but it focuses on the emotional nature of relationships within the system. There are many good resources in print and online as to how to do a genogram. Be warned, this will require you to have as many conversations as possible with people in your family of origin and this can be anxiety producing in its own right. By doing this, you will be taking the first step toward reworking the unresolved relationships in your life. You can also attend workshops or take courses that will help you to do this. Consult the appendix for a list of resources. Many people have done their own work by taking the initiative to learn about family systems, to gain perspective about their family of origin from its own members and to rework the anxiety producing relationships in their lives. I am one of them.

The important thing is to do your own work. Nobody can do it for you. That's how you move forward.

It's Process NOT Content

It's process NOT content.

It's PROCESS not content.

It's process not CONTENT.

I find myself saying this often when working with church leaders, either individually or in groups. It is a family systems mantra that is critical to developing as a person and a leader.

Friedman describes it in a more oblique way: Nobody gets the problem they can handle. What is a problem for one family is no big deal to another. In one family, a kid can come home with all A's and a C on her report card, and she'll get grounded for the C. In another, she might come home with all C's and an A, and they are celebrating the success of an A. For the former, a C is a problem. For the latter, it's not. But the latter family will typically have something that IS a problem. For example, if the daughter doesn't make the varsity softball team in 10th grade, it might seem like the end of the world.

In each problem situation, the process is similar, but the content is different. In these examples, the process is the anxiety and upset that occurs. The content is grades or sports. But the content could be anything. Nobody gets the problem they can handle, because it is our own reaction, our own software that makes it a problem in the first place.

A problem is different than a challenge. Life is about challenges, because life is hard. We often rise to the occasion and work our way through the challenge, which results in personal growth. A problem is a challenge that we are struggling to handle effectively. And that has more to do with us than the challenge. Maybe we feel ill-equipped and helpless. Are we really? Maybe we are angry at what has happened and act out in harmful ways. Does the acting out change things? Nobody gets the problem they can handle. Otherwise it wouldn't be a problem.

Back to process and content. A family systems view helps us to look at our interactions to understand what is going on in the system and with others. For example, in a church meeting, people can disagree in any number of ways. They can self-differentiate, using "I" statements in a non-anxious way. They can self-define, but not engage (narcissism). They can spew anxiety at everyone in sight. They can clam up and not take a stand at all, even if they disagree. Notice that I haven't named a topic or issue. That would be content, and content is irrelevant from a leadership standpoint. What's important is that the way people respond helps us to understand the processes at work in the system. And understanding these processes can help us to be most effective as a leader.

I've often been asked if self-differentiation means I don't want to listen to what others are saying. That couldn't be further from the truth. It's important to listen to what others say, because I might be wrong. If I am not listening, I am the one with the problem. But it's HOW they are saying it (process) that's the issue more than WHAT they are saying (content). If I am self-differentiating and someone responds with lots of anxiety and blaming, then I am thinking two things. First, I am not the issue. She is displacing pain from another part of her life, and I happen to be the current target. Second, because I am not the issue and the content is just her excuse to vent, I am not likely to convince her to agree with me. We humans aren't easily swayed in our opinions. We are even more obstinate when our positions are not rational. My approach is more likely to be a non-anxious presence. To not get defensive, to not argue content, but to stay connected emotionally. How that's done will be explained in Chapter 8. For now, it's essential to understand the difference between process and content.

Someone else might make the same points in a self-defined, non-anxious way. We can have a conversation. Again, it's best for me to avoid being defensive and to continue to self-define. But I will engage in discussing the content, because the process that is occurring tells me that the other is expressing herself in a healthy way. I can work with that.

As we dig deeper into leadership through differentiation, learning to recognize process becomes a critical skill. It will help you become more aware of what is happening and enable you to develop a repertoire of responses that can move the system forward. Nowhere is understanding process more important than with emotional triangles. If self-differentiation is the key, then unlocking emotional triangles is the process that leads to a healthier, more effective family, church or organization. Let's look at that next.

Chapter 3
Unlocking Emotional Triangles

Emotional triangles carry a paradox. The process by which they function is the major force that keeps systems stuck in chronic patterns of dysfunction. Yet unlocking them is the primary way that you, as a leader, can effect significant change. As we'll see, this has more to do with your own functioning and has nothing to do with trying to change others. You can only be responsible for yourself. But the more you do that, while staying connected emotionally, the more likely it is that others will change in positive ways. To do this, you need to understand how emotional triangles work.

Understanding Emotional Triangles

An emotional triangle requires three sides or legs. By definition, two of the sides are uncomfortable with their relationship and will focus on the third side to stabilize the relationship with each other. By triangling the third, they avoid dealing with each other. The third side of the triangle does not have to be a person; it can also be an issue, such as substance abuse, infidelity or over-investment at work.

A typical example of a triangle is a marriage where the two spouses are uncomfortable with one another and one spouse focuses on a child as a way to stabilize the relationship. The focus on the child is more intense from this spouse than the other. The general idea is that it diverts emotional energy from the uncomfortable relationship between the spouses. The more intense parent will tend to overfunction with the child, while the less intense parent will tend to underfunction.

The focus can appear positive. The spouse might invest heavily in the child's success. It could be academics, sports, music, art, hunting, fishing or any number of areas. It goes beyond encouraging the child to grow in ability and capacity. It is an intense emotional investment by which the parent is living vicariously through the child and/or whose own sense of well-being is wrapped up in the child's success. The focus can also appear to be negative. This is especially true when the child starts to develop symptoms that are likely because the child has no capacity to self-differentiate. Her parents haven't modeled self-differentiation, so she doesn't know how to take a non-anxious, emotional stand with the more intense parent. This most often occurs as "acting out," doing poorly in school, rebellious behavior, drug and alcohol use, etc. There are two important process points demonstrated by this.

The first is that the third leg of a triangle can be either a person or an issue. In this example, the acting out (an issue) becomes the third leg of the triangle. It is the child's way of dealing with her uncomfortable relationship with the intense parent. It is an effort, mostly subconscious, by the child to get the focus off herself. The intense parent will likely respond with anxiety, focusing on the issue and the child's functioning, rather than focusing on her own functioning.

The second point about triangles and emotional process is that triangles interlock. In the example, there is a triangle between the spouses and the child, as well as a triangle between the intense parent, the child and the issue of acting out. A classic triangle interlock in the traditional family is a couple who is uncomfortable with each other emotionally. There is a triangle between the two spouses and the man's career with a heavy investment in his work. Then there is a triangle between the man, the woman and her child, as described above. As gender roles change, this particular set of triangles may seem less likely, but it will still occur. It may be the stay-at-home dad who over-invests in the child and the mom who over-invests in her career. Regardless, whenever two spouses or partners are uncomfortable in their relationship, regardless of gender, triangles are likely to occur. Remember: it's process, not content.

The existence of triangles in any system is due to the inherent instability in a two-person relationship. Unless both persons are very self-differentiated, there is likely to be discomfort at some level. If the best we can hope for is 70% differentiation, and that's when we are functioning at our best, then most of us are likely to be in relationships that get uncomfortable. The question is: When it gets uncomfortable, do we respond as a non-anxious presence, or do we triangle a third person or issue?

Friedman describes a hypothetical couple who are both functioning at 100% self-differentiation:

"Each could move toward or away from the other in separate, disengaged movements. If the husband said he was going to the movies, his wife would not be insulted if she were not invited. Or, if he asked her to go along she could feel free to say no and he could still go. There would be a maximum of 'I' statements defining position, rather than blaming 'you,' statements that hold the other responsible for their own condition or destiny. At times, the partners might appear to be disconnected. But there is nothing internally wrong with the way they are connected, nothing to keep them from being close one minute or separating another minute, with minimum tugging on each other."[1]

Yes... this is a fantasy. But it describes what 100% differentiation looks like in a relationship. Most of us would do well to be at 50%. The point is this: the lower two persons are on the scale of differentiation, the more inherently unstable the relationship is likely to be and the more likely triangles will form to stabilize the relationship.

You can't change a relationship to which you do not belong (repeat, take a deep breath, and repeat). This is essential to understanding how triangles work. Most of us, when in a triangle, will try to change the relationship of the other two. This has two results. The first is that our efforts will cause the relationship to go in the opposite direction. Let's go back to the family example. In this case, it's the dad who is over-invested in their son.

The child starts acting out, and the overinvolved parent might say, "You need to do something about your child!"

The child is likely to go to the under-involved parent and say, "Can you get dad off my back? He's always on my case about 'fill in the blank' (process, not content)."

In this situation, most of us will try to "fix" the relationship between the other two. "Well he's a good kid, you know. Why don't you try to understand him better." And, "Your dad just cares about you, son. Try to put yourself in his shoes." This increases the chances that the triangle will strengthen, either because they focus their anger on the under-involved parent or because they start taking sides against her.

The second result of trying to change the relationship of two other people is it causes you to take on the stress of the other relationship. Either because you are overfunctioning by trying to get them to get along better, or because they will focus their emotions on you to stabilize their own relationship. In either case, you will be the one that carries the most stress.

There is a "stuckness" to triangles. One side of the triangle tends to have more conflict than the other two sides. Conflict is unavoidable in relationships. In healthy families, there is a randomness to conflict. One time it may be between parents, another time between a parent and a child, and another time between two siblings. A sure sign of a triangle is when the conflict most often occurs between the same two people. That doesn't mean that conflict won't occur on the other sides of the triangle, it just means that it will occur more often on the same side. Back to our example: When the son starts acting out, it's likely that conflict will escalate between the parents. That's the side that was uncomfortable to begin with. The spouses may have appeared to get along, because of the father's intense investment in the child. But when junior starts acting out, because of the nature of the triangle, the parents are more likely to blame each other than to make junior responsible for his actions.

Triangles can also occur when one person in an uncomfortable relationship creates false companionship with a third person, usually through secrets and gossip. The person on the outside will hardly know what is going on, but the very nature of the triangle will create stress. The false companionship, secrets and gossip create emotional distance between the two insiders and the one on the outside, making her feel even more cut off, without knowing why. Whenever someone comes to you and says, "Don't tell so-and-so, but...," it is likely that they are uncomfortable with their relationship with so-and-so and that they are seeking you as a false companion.

Triangles and the Church

What makes triangles so powerful in the church is that the church is a family system of family systems. Not only are there triangles within the church, but there are triangles that connect individual families and the church.

Here are some examples of triangles within the church. In each case, the first two persons or issues have the uncomfortable relationship, and the third is the focus of their emotional energy (the one being triangled) to stabilize their relationship:

- The choir director and a church member each complain to the pastor about the other

- A church member, the budget (financial problems) and blame displacement toward the denomination

- A church member, grief over the leaving of a previous pastor and blame displacement toward the current pastor

- The pastor, a staff member and the staff member confiding secrets about the pastor with a church member

- The pastor, congregation and the pastor's feelings of responsibility for their salvation

Here are examples of triangles that connect individual families with the church:

- A church member, a conflict with a son and the church member's criticism of the lay leader

- A woman, her husband who doesn't come to church and her criticism of the worship service

- A man, unresolved issues with his brother and his overinvestment in committee work at church

- A church member, grief over a dying spouse and anger at the pastor for not doing enough

And, finally, here are examples of triangles that connect the pastor's family and the church:

- The pastor, spouse and pastor's over-investment in the ministry

- The pastor, congregation and their complaints about the pastor's kids

- The pastor, congregation and complaints about the spouse's involvement at church

Yes, it's a mess. But the existence of triangles is a double-edged sword. They can keep a system stuck. But if a leader, and, in particular, the pastor, can maintain self-differentiated positions in these triangles, she can unlock the triangles and move the system toward better health and effectiveness.

Self-Differentiation as the Key

The forces that hold interlocking triangles together in any system can be reversed through a consistent, self-differentiated presence. The initial response will be sabotage. The system will push back, making it even more difficult for the leader to maintain a non-anxious presence. However, if she can continue in this way, the forces will flip and start to create pressure on others to self-differentiate. Over time, the system can find a new equilibrium that is much healthier and emotionally mature. Chapter 7 deals with sabotage and how to maintain a non-anxious presence. For now, let's look at how self-differentiation is the key.

The way to unlock a triangle is to give back the other two persons the responsibility for their relationship; or, if the other side is a person and her issue, to give her back responsibility for her issue. It's not like you wrap responsibility in a box, put a bow on it, then say, "Here, I give you back responsibility for your own problems." But that's not a bad way to think of it. In reality, by definition, you give people responsibility for their own stuff by maintaining a non-anxious presence, by being self-differentiated. As a self-differentiated person, you take responsibility for your own emotional functioning, but not for that of others.

When you are not self-differentiating, a triangle can make you feel compelled to overfunction. Let's say you are the pastor or lay leader in a congregation. Two other members have a conflictual relationship, but they won't deal with each other. Instead, they each come to you individually and complain about the other. They beg you or threaten you to do something about the other. The issue at hand could be anything.

"He doesn't know how to run a meeting."

"She plays hymns too fast."

"He doesn't pull his weight on trustees."

"She rules the Sunday School with an iron fist."

The issue is irrelevant. It's process, not content. Whether they ask explicitly or not, by triangling you they are asking you to take responsibility for the relationship, which usually means to "fix" the other. But you can only change a relationship to which you belong. And their relationship is their problem.

Here is what most people would say: "How about if the three of us sit down and talk about it?" Stop! Noooooooo! This is classic overfunctioning. If you do this, you will be sitting in the meeting, and they are going to put more pressure on you to fix the other person. Or you'll spend a lot of time talking about the "issue," which is not really the problem. The problem is their inability to deal with their uncomfortable relationship, which is why they triangled you in the first place. Alternatively, you might try to talk to each of them individually to help them to get along better or to see the other person's perspective. Again, stop it! You are not responsible for their relationship and are not the one who can change it. Only they can do that. The more you try to do it, the more stress you will feel.

The way out is to self-differentiate. To be a non-anxious presence. To stay connected emotionally, but to only take responsibility for your own functioning. You don't do this with them together; you do it in your interactions with each one individually. This is hard. You WILL feel anxious. But the more you do your own work, and the more you learn to self-differentiate, the better you will get at being a non-anxious presence.

When I first entered pastoral ministry, I was a "student-pastor." I was attending seminary, but I was also the pastor of a small church. I also was married with three young children and a fourth on the way. Needless to say, life was busy. About midway through my first year, the person who had been doing the monthly church newsletter for years decided to resign. Nobody stepped up immediately to do it. We asked around and put announcements in the bulletin, but nobody volunteered. People started saying to me, "Boy we sure miss the newsletter," or, "People are saying they sure miss the newsletter." When you hear "people are saying," run! Talk about surrounding togetherness pressure.

So here's the triangle: the congregation, the lack of the newsletter (issue) and me. They were trying to triangle me into taking responsibility for the newsletter. But I was having trouble keeping up with my own life, so it never even entered my mind to try to do it. Sometimes it's good to be dense. The other unhealthy response, besides actually doing the newsletter myself, would have been to get defensive. "You aren't asking me to do the newsletter, are you? I just can't do it. I don't have the time. That's really unreasonable of you." (Uh oh, I just started blaming.) It's process, not content. (Have I said this enough?) Whenever you start arguing content in a triangle, you are sunk.

Anyway, I saw the newsletter as their responsibility, so my answer to their comments was, "I miss the newsletter, too."

I stayed connected emotionally, and I self-defined. Like I said, I was dense, so it was not a conscious attempt to self-differentiate. It's better to be lucky than good. After about six months of this, two people in the congregation decided that they would work together to do the newsletter. One would collect the content; the other would do the layout. Voilà. No more triangle.

This is a good time to discuss the concept of pain and responsibility. The problem most of us have is that we have a low threshold for others' pain. We want to relieve them of their pain. However, pain is an opportunity for growth. The cliché, "no pain, no gain," is true. If you can increase your ability to tolerate the pain of others, you can give them a chance to grow.

In my example, the congregation was feeling the pain of not having a newsletter. If I had been less dense, I might have felt the need to relieve them of their pain and have done the newsletter. But that would strengthen the triangle and make it almost permanent. The congregation could proudly say, "Here comes the newsletter editor. Oh, he's also our pastor." How long do you think it would take to get someone to do the newsletter once I started doing it? And how many other congregational responsibilities would I end up taking on?

Which brings up the other side of the pain and responsibility coin. You want people to be responsible, but you can't make them responsible. In fact, trying to make someone responsible is more likely to make them LESS responsible. The way to help someone become more responsible is to allow them to suffer the consequences of their actions. This requires you to have a higher tolerance for THEIR pain. When you overfunction, you make the other less capable of taking responsibility. The ultimate goal of giving someone back their pain is to increase their capacity to handle a challenge. A challenge is only a problem if they can't handle it. Increased pain thresholds lead to increased ability to take responsibility, which leads to increased capacity to handle challenges. The congregation needed to feel their pain over not having a newsletter. That was the healthy way out.

I mentioned another way that being triangled can affect you: you get defensive. This is especially true if the other two are displacing blame on you. That is, instead of asking you to fix their relationship, they are blaming you for the way they feel and for not doing something about it.

Here's a hypothetical example. A church member comes to you and says, "Our organist plays the hymns way too slowly. If you would just do your job as a leader, this wouldn't happen." You could overfunction and say to the organist, "People are saying (shame on you) that you're playing the hymns too slowly." This is overfunctioning, because you are doing exactly what the complaining church member is unable to do. Or you can get defensive. You can respond to the accusation by saying, "What do you mean? I think I'm a good leader. I really try hard to keep everybody happy. I'm diligent, responsible, and I have great faith." While the presence of "I" statements seems like you're self-defining, you are arguing content (your leadership capability), and that's a trap. It keeps the focus on you and helps the other to avoid taking responsibility for her own condition. Worse yet, you could counterattack. "You're one to talk. You only come to church half the time, and you think you have the right to criticize the organist." When people come looking for a fight they are displacing some other pain and blaming you. Fighting back will keep them angry at you and won't help them to take responsibility for themselves. Whether you overfunction or get defensive, you will take on the stress of the triangle.

So what do you do? Here are four approaches.

1. Use paradox and playfulness. According to family systems theory, there is a paradox to seriousness. You need to take life seriously, but the more serious you are, especially as measured by anxiety, the less likely you are to be able to handle the situation. When you are too serious, too anxious, challenge becomes a problem. And nobody gets the problem they can handle.

    Playfulness is paradoxical. It is counterintuitive. When super-serious others flail their anxiety at you, your instinct is to get serious and try to fix things, either through overfunctioning or defensiveness. Playfulness lightens the mood. It turns the thermostat down a few notches and helps to dissipate anxiety. It avoids arguing content without blaming and in a non-anxious way.

    Here's a playful response, "I thought all the songs in the hymnal were supposed to sound like dirges." It doesn't argue content, isn't defensive and is a bit humorous (at least I think so). But playfulness is hard to pull off. If it comes off as sarcasm, then don't do it. Playfulness works, but it's most often effective when you know what's coming and you can prepare yourself for it. Playfulness is effective, not because it's some kind of ninja mind trick on the other. It's effective because it keeps YOU from getting too serious, from overfunctioning or getting defensive. It's process, not content.

2. Give back the problem, literally. In this case, you would go to the organist and say, "You know what so-and-so said? She thinks that you play hymns way too slowly. Hey, I'm not agreeing with her, I just thought you should know." Of course, so-and-so may not be too happy and may confront you. You will feel anxious. But if you can remain a non-anxious presence, then you can dissipate your anxiety and possibly theirs. When

confronted, you can say, "That's just how I roll. I like to keep everything out in the open."

When giving back the problem, it's helpful to understand the destructive nature of secrets and gossip. When someone comes to you with secrets and gossip it is, by its very nature, an effort to triangle you. They are uncomfortable with their relationship with the other and by coming to you with a secret or gossip about them they are triangling you. Furthermore, they make it nearly impossible to have healthy interactions. Secrets divide the system into insiders and outsiders. They create false companionship among the insiders and estrangement between insiders and outsiders. Most importantly, secrets increase the anxiety level of the entire system. Think about a time when someone told you a secret and then you were faced with dealing with the person from whom you were to keep the secret. Did you feel anxious? Of course. Multiply that throughout the system and you understand what secrets can do. So, in our example, so-and-so might be upset. The organist might be upset at hearing what so-and-so thinks. But if you can maintain a non-anxious presence, they will get over it. And perhaps even deal with it. The reason we keep secrets is because we are trying to spare others from getting upset. But, as Friedman writes: "Few of us are irreparably hurt by upset. Chronic anxiety, on the other hand, kills."[2]

I'm often asked, "But Pastor Jack, aren't we supposed to maintain confidentiality?" Yes, we are. But there is a difference between confidentiality and a secret. My rule of thumb: when a person is talking about herself, then there may be confidentiality. When she is talking about another, it is possibly a secret or gossip. And the better you get at not keeping secrets, the less often you will be triangled in this way. Multiply the organist example a few times, and people will know that if they come to you about another, the other is going to hear about it.

Once I had a person who knew me well come to me and say, "I'm going to tell you something about so-and-so, but you can't tell her about it." I just stared at him and smiled. He said, "You're going to tell her, aren't you?"

I nodded and said, "Of course I will."

So he responded, "Then I'm not telling you."

"OK," I said.

Awkward silence.

We both laughed and he got up and left.

Once people know you won't keep secrets, they will stop telling them to you.

3. Simply say, "I need to pray about this." It buys you some time. It keeps you from having to respond right away with your own anxiety. It helps you to stay connected emotionally. If you do this, you need to be prepared to get back to the person in some way that is self-differentiated and non-anxious. Otherwise you just copped out, and the triangle will persist. In our example, you could tell the organist, then go back to so-and-so and say, "I prayed about it and decided to tell the organist what you said." Or you could triangle God and say, "God told me to tell the organist." But that would not be taking responsibility for your own position. Either way, praying about it is a good thing. You probably ought to do that no matter what. But it's not replacement for leadership through self-differentiation. It WILL help you prepare better.

4. The final approach to being triangled is to ask questions. Listening helps you to remain non-anxious, because, as long as you don't respond, you don't have to take an

emotional stand. Just keep asking open-ended questions. What makes you say that? How long have you felt this way? How are you coping with it? Sometimes people just want to vent and this is enough. I've often done this, and the other will say, "Thanks for letting me vent," and that's the end of it. By definition, listening is also staying emotionally connected, because you are showing interest and care in the other's situation. If the other doesn't end it herself, you can say, "Thanks for sharing." You can offer to pray for her. You may or may not need to follow up, depending on the intensity of her demands, but asking questions definitely will help you dissipate the anxiety in the moment.

Emotional triangles are a fact of life in any relationship system. You cannot avoid them. Leadership through self-differentiation is the key to unlocking triangles. There is no place where triangles are more prevalent than in an anxious church. The next chapter helps you to identify what that looks like.

Chapter 4
An Anxious Church

It's not surprising, in an age of anxiety, that many Christians worship in an anxious church. Mainline Protestantism has experienced a steady decline in membership and attendance over the last few decades. One clergy colleague said to me: "When people come to church on Sunday morning they are filled with anxiety by the empty pews that they see. They may not think about it during the week, but they are reminded as soon as they enter on Sunday. We used to preach into the anxiety in their lives. Now it seems like we need to preach into their anxiety over the church."

This kind of anxiety can be evident in any church that has experienced decline. An anxious church is different. It has particular kinds of dysfunction that make it exceptionally difficult for leaders to effect positive change. In *A Failure of Nerve*, Friedman identified five characteristics of a chronically anxious family: reactivity, herding, blame displacement, a quick-fix mentality and a lack of well-differentiated leadership.[1] Let's examine what these characteristics look like in an anxious church.

Reactivity

Reactivity is different than disagreement. The latter is natural and, when done properly, is healthy for any family or organization. Disagreements lead to individuals exchanging ideas and perspectives, tossing out ideas and using different perspectives to carve a way forward. Reactivity, however, is fueled by anxiety. Reactivity can reject any attempts at changing the status quo, it can balk at change and it wildly looks to assign blame on others rather than finding a solution.

For example, if a church council is considering a big decision, it is entirely appropriate for someone to say, "I just don't agree with what was just said. I believe that…" On the other hand, someone might say, rather intensely, "That's just wrong. You all know better than that. If we do that, we'll all be sorry. We just don't have a chance with all the things that are going on out there." In the "I" statement, the speaker is owning up to her responsibility and creating the space to make things better. But a "you" statement assigns blame and stops progress. If you are more likely to hear the latter than the former, you are probably in an anxious church.

One clue to identifying reactivity is the lack of "I" statements. When people use "you" and "we," it's a sign that they are refusing to take responsibility for the issue. "I" statements take responsibility for self, while "you" statements often infer blame. When used in a reactive way, they are blaming others for one's own condition. When people feel blamed, they can get defensive and resentful, heightening the anxiety in the interaction.

In the 1960's, psychologist Thomas Gordon coined the term "I" statement. There are three components in Gordon's model:

1. A non-blaming description of the offending behavior

2. How it makes you feel

3. How the behavior affects you

But, as John A. Johnson points out in his *Psychology Today* article, "Are 'I' Statements Better than 'You' Statements?,"[2] even certain "I" statements can feel like blaming. Johnson turns Gordon's model on its head.

"Here is one of the examples used to demonstrate the three essential components: 'I feel very upset [FEELINGS] when you're not here at 8:30 a.m. to answer the phone [BEHAVIOR] because that means I have to leave my work to cover for you [EFFECT].'

The paradox lies in the assertion that the person using the 'I' statement is allegedly not blaming the other person's behavior for his or her unhappiness, but at the same time is saying that the behavior is causing an undesirable, unacceptable effect on the speaker. Blaming is the act of claiming that someone's behavior is the cause of my unhappiness. So, despite taking some of the focus off of the other person by saying 'I feel very upset' instead of 'Your tardiness is upsetting me,' in the end the speaker is still blaming the receptionist's tardiness for his or her upset feelings. So, it seems to me that I-Statements with all three essential components cannot be non-blameful."[3]

Johnson's point is that even most "I" statements can come across as blaming. One thing an "I" statement may tell you is that the speaker is self-aware enough to try to blame you for her condition in a non-threatening way. Ironically, Johnson gives an example of an "I" statement that really does take responsibility for one's own feelings, without blaming, but he seems to do it with tongue-in-cheek.

"If an I-Statement were truly non-blameful, it would look more like this: 'When I am the only one here and I have to cover the phone, I get really upset. But, hey, that's my problem. I am telling myself that it is a horrible thing to be answering the phone instead of doing other work, but this is just irrational, limiting self-talk. I am 'awfulizing' -- magnifying the problem beyond all proportion. I need to take responsibility for my own feelings by monitoring and adjusting my self-talk."[4]

While Johnson may be kidding, this is exactly what self-differentiation looks like. It is non-anxious, non-blaming and takes responsibility for self while staying emotionally connected. We will look at why this works in greater depth.

What's important to understand here is that even when someone is in the wrong, it doesn't mean that they will take constructive criticism well. In Johnson's example, it's quite possible that using a traditional "I" statement will still get a negative reaction from the tardy one, because she will experience it as being accused or criticized. My experience is that most people don't handle being told they are wrong very well. They get defensive and can even go on the attack. That's what reactivity is. What is counterintuitive about self-differentiation is that it doesn't even hint at blaming. It says, "Hey, this is my problem." Even though, in this example, the problem is caused by the receptionist. And, even if you make a self-differentiated statement, like Johnson's tongue-in-cheek example, you may still get blasted. That's reactivity. Blaming another for one's own condition is a characteristic of reactivity.

"We" statements are a much clearer example of reactivity. They imply that we all need to fall in line or else. Remember that self-differentiation is defined as the ability to define one's own goals and values in the midst of surrounding togetherness pressures. "We" statements epitomize surrounding togetherness pressures. When I say, "We need to offer a contemporary service," it means that I know best and you need to go along. "We" statements invite you to agree or keep quiet. They create surrounding togetherness pressures. If I say, "I believe offering a contemporary service would be a great idea," then I'm taking responsibility for my own position without requiring you to agree with me. That's leadership through self-differentiation.

"We" statements, like "I" statements, are often a "you" statement in disguise. When someone says to you, "We need to do something about the music in this church," they might really be saying that YOU need to do something. It is a refusal to take responsibility and an attempt to put the responsibility on you.

The common element in all these statements is the refusal to take responsibility and/or the blaming of another for one's own condition. This is both a sign of reactivity and fuel for the anxiety in the system. At the root of the response is anxiety, which is not always evident. A reactive response can be said in a calm manner, but it is reactive just the same. However, it's not unusual for the reactive response to be anything but calm, which makes it easier to identify. When one is spewing anxiety at everyone around them, it's a pretty good indication of a reactive response.

Reactivity can also take a different and more pernicious form called adaptive behavior. Adaptive behavior is the opposite of self-definition. It allows the other, whether an individual or a group, to define one's position. In the case of a church decision, the adaptive response would be to go along with whatever is decided. There is still anxiety. In the adaptive person, the anxiety is stuffed so as not to disturb the situation, but the anxiety can't be stuffed forever.

The anxiety in an adaptive person will ultimately be released in one of three ways. One is through an eruption of anxious reactivity. Like a volcano, all the anxiety comes spewing out with intense emotions of anger and blaming. The second is through passive aggressive behavior. There is apparent agreement with the other, but one actually doesn't go along and may actually subvert what is agreed to. Finally, there is triangling. Remember, a triangle occurs when two persons experience discomfort in their relationship and focus on a third person or issue to stabilize their relationship.

Adaptive behavior can take the form of a triangle. When a relationship gets uncomfortable, one of the persons can agree with the other, rather than saying how they feel. This is adaptive behavior because they are "adapting" to the other person, rather than dealing with the discomfort by taking a stand. If they release one's discomfort by expressing it to a third person, that is triangling. For example, a congregant may be uncomfortable with the pastor and unable to say what she feels. She just agrees with the pastor, but then she complains to the choir director. The anxiety that the congregant feels because she is unable to take a stand with her pastor is released by triangling the choir director. It's not healthy for the congregant or the church.

These three forms of anxiety release are not mutually exclusive. One can be passive aggressive for a time, then erupt. Or one can be passive aggressive AND form a triangle. Doesn't that sound like fun? One can form a triangle, but that won't necessarily prevent an anxiety eruption.

What makes adaptive behavior more pernicious is that it is harder to identify. Eruptions can be few and far between. Passive aggressive behavior is not always evident. Triangles, and the secretive behavior that can accompany them, are not always evident either. That being said, the best clue to adaptive behavior is when a person rarely, if ever, defines her own position. In a system, whether family, church or organization, if a person always goes along with what others say without ever expressing her own beliefs, then it likely is adaptive behavior.

Reactivity, whether adaptive or reactive, is the first sign of an anxious family, church or organization. Some references to the former will use the term "adaptive reactivity," as a reminder that adapting is a form of reactivity.

Herding

Surrounding togetherness pressures are the forces that create herding in families, churches and organizations. They are a byproduct of reactivity in anxious systems. Defining one's own goals and values is being able to take a stand while staying emotionally connected with others, even in the midst of those pressures.

As noted in the last chapter, a good place to see surrounding togetherness pressures is to observe how families handle holidays. Anxious families have an unseen force that dictates what will happen and that everyone must comply. If a family member decides to buck family tradition and spend their holiday away from the family, or if they choose not to participate in family events, there is a great deal of pushback and an escalation of anxiety. On the other hand, in less anxious families, people feel freer to self-define. One example is saying, "I'm going to spend Christmas with my spouse's family this year," without fear of starting any "family drama." Anyone who has had a significant other or spouse has likely dealt with surrounding togetherness pressures.

Herding, by its very nature, is against self-differentiation. It discourages people from defining their own position. When one does try to define a position, there is a reactive response. For example, I was once in a church that had a kitchen where we prepared meals for fellowship events and fundraising dinners. As we were prepping for a roast beef dinner at the church, it was decided the meat slicer was no longer needed for the dinner. In previous years, the meat was cooked in the church kitchen, but this year a church member who owned a restaurant had volunteered to cook and slice the roast beef, then deliver it to the church. Word got around that some members of the church decided that the meat slicer could be moved into the closet for the dinner so there would be more counter space in the kitchen. It wasn't long after that the following note was mysteriously taped to the meat slicer:

"By order of the Kitchen Committee, the meat slicer shall not be moved."

The meat slicer stayed in the kitchen for the roast beef dinner.

There is a circular nature to herding. Surrounding togetherness pressures result from reactivity. The anxious nature of the system causes people to fear taking emotional stands. People are afraid to say, "This is what I believe," when it disagrees with the surrounding togetherness pressures. That results in everyone falling in line. The more surrounding togetherness pressures grow, the more anxious, and thereby reactive, the system becomes. The more reactive the system becomes, the more pressure there is to conform and not self-define.

This circular nature results in the system adapting to the least mature member. In an anxious system there are few self-differentiated persons; because of this, the squeaky wheel gets the oil. In a family, this might be the alcoholic, the philanderer, the delinquent, the hothead, etc. The common element is the reactive or adaptive response of others in the system. There is yelling, nagging or lecturing (reactivity), none of which are helpful and are more likely to cause the least mature member to be resentful and feel more justified in acting out. Or there is enabling behavior (adaptivity), which, instead of calling the least mature to be accountable, actually facilitates their acting out. This perpetuates immature behavior. In either case, anxiety is pervasive and surrounding togetherness pressures cause people to conform.

An anxious church will exhibit herding behavior, which includes adaptation to the least mature member or members. There is typically a person or group that is throwing a fit, sulking or feeling hurt. This makes everyone else feel anxious and promotes reactive behavior. Sometimes this can result in heated battles (reactivity). I have more often seen that others, including the pastor and church leaders, are afraid to self-define (adaptivity), so they go along.

The actual issue that causes the problem will vary all over the map. It can be the color of the carpet, how often the pastor takes off or whether the family that volunteers to clean the church should provide the toilet paper at their own expense. The possible issues are infinite, but the process is the same. The most immature, that is, least self-differentiated, rule, either overtly or covertly. If self-differentiated persons take responsibility for their own condition, the most immature do exactly the opposite, blaming others and refusing to take responsibility. Everyone feels anxious and everyone must go along. That is herding.

Blame Displacement

Blame displacement is blaming outside forces for one's own condition. It avoids taking responsibility for one's own well-being and destiny. Blame displacement results in feeling victimized and helpless. It is the opposite of looking inward for emotional resources to respond to challenges.

For example, a family might focus on the prevalence of sex and violence in the media. They rant and rave about Hollywood producers and their lack of morals. They get irate over lyrics in popular music. They rant because primetime TV contains sexually explicit topics and images. The focus is on what is wrong with external conditions, and it leads to a sense of helplessness. The family's response is likely to "hunker down" and try to provide a protective shield around their children. The parents screen every song, video game, TV show and movie to keep their kids from exposure to any debauchery. They ensure that their kids' smartphones are void of any explicit material or risky apps.

The parents may be correct in their assessment, according to their own values. What they find in the media may truly offend them, but the problem is blame displacement. It puts the focus on the outside forces instead of on their own response. There is nothing wrong with restricting a child's media consumption. It's certainly within the purview of parenting. But the external focus diminishes their own resources and, worse yet, teaches their children to feel victimized. Let's look at two different responses.

The blame displacement response would typically elicit statements like, "The media is corrupt, and their agenda is to bring children over to their side. It's my job to protect you from this kind of evil." The focus is on the outside force and not one's own resources to respond. A self-differentiated response would be, "I don't like what I see in the media. It goes against my values and the values I'm trying to raise you with." The difference is the defining of self and taking responsibility for one's own condition.

Let's say that in either case the parent is restricting media consumption. This is well and good, but eventually there will be a "breach," for example during primetime TV, when something shows up that they couldn't filter. Examining responses to this "breach" helps to further understand blame displacement. An external focus would be, "I can't believe they let that kind of smut on TV at 8 p.m.! They are trying to pollute your mind!" A self-differentiated response would be, "I'm very disappointed that this is shown at 8 p.m." Then, to the child, "I think we should discuss what we just saw and why it concerns me." Which child do you think will be better prepared to deal with challenge in life?

Pointing to external circumstances as an insurmountable obstacle is, by its very nature, not taking responsibility for the problem. Blaming outside forces may be an accurate assessment of what is causing the problem, but it abandons any personal responsibility. For example, when someone says about the flourishing new church down the street, "I don't know why the denomination let them start a new church right down the street. We're never going to grow now," this not only creates anxiety, but it also fosters a sense of helplessness, making the assertion true. With this kind of anxiety, it was likely they were never going to grow anyway. An anxious church has an external focus on the cause of its problems.

You will hear statements such as:

> "If we didn't have to pay to support our denominational structure, we wouldn't have money problems."

> "If the soccer leagues wouldn't schedule games on Sundays, we'd have more young families."

> "That non-denominational church down the street is taking all our members."

The chronically anxious church has an outward focus on its problems (blame displacement) and an inward focus on care and concern. Members complain about outside factors and will focus their resources on taking care of those already in the church. They take responsibility for each other, but not for the church's problems. This perpetuates feelings of being victimized and of helplessness.

On the other hand, a spiritually healthy church has an inward focus on spiritual and emotional resources and an outward focus on care and concern for those in need. They take responsibility for their relationship with God and for their own spiritual growth. They take responsibility, individually and collectively, for how they respond to the inevitable challenges that the church will face. Likewise, because they trust in the spiritual and emotional resources that come from God, they feel led to reach out and serve those in need in the community. They don't do this to get new members or to solve their problems. They do this as an expression of who they are. They don't feel like victims or feel helpless. They feel empowered by God.

What kind of church are you leading?

Quick Fix Mentality

A quick fix mentality seeks immediate symptom relief instead of going through the longer, more painful process of fundamental change. One characteristic is a low threshold for emotional pain. Working through emotional pain is how we grow and progress in life. People with a low pain threshold will avoid facing their pain and the accompanying possibility for positive change. Instead, they will seek the quick fix.

Let's say that the person showing symptoms in a chronically anxious family is dealing with addiction. The typical response of the family would be to seek as much professional help as possible. Rehab centers, therapists and doctors will all be sought to take care of the problem. Immediate professional help is not unreasonable. Yet, the chronically anxious family would view this "quick fix" as THE answer.

A family systems approach would ask the questions: "How is my own functioning contributing to this issue? How can I change my own behavior, that is, my input into the system, to help us work toward long-term improvement?" This latter approach acknowledges that the addicted one is carrying the symptoms for the system and that a quick fix is never a real fix. When the focus is all on the symptom-bearer, the rest of the family avoids taking responsibility for their own behavior. There may be temporary relief, but it's just that -- temporary. Rehab can help start the healing process, but unless at least one other person changes her behavior (input into the system), things will return to their original condition. This is the cycle of rehab -- temporary freedom from addiction, a slide back into addictive behavior, then rehab again.

The reason groups like Al-Anon are so important is that they help others in the system focus on their own input. They help them deal with their own emotional pain. They help family members take responsibility for their own functioning and avoid seeking the quick fix.

The quick fix mentality and blame displacement are opposite sides of the same coin. Both are focused on external forces: one to quickly fix the problem; the other to identify blame for the problem. Both help avoid responsibility for one's own emotional resources and functioning. They are the antithesis of dealing with challenge to facilitate personal growth. The anxious church is no different. The symptoms will be different, but the process is the same. It is characterized by a desire for certainty and the unwillingness to endure the challenge and change that are required for growth. Ironically, it is this pain avoidance that results in chronic anxiety.

Not all churches that have experienced a long-term decline in attendance are anxious. Demographic trends have affected most mainline Protestant churches. However, virtually all anxious churches have experienced this decline. They can't get out of their own way. A quick fix mentality ensures this.

One example of a quick fix mentality in the anxious church is throwing a great deal of church resources and faith into the latest, greatest program to turn things around in the church. Sometimes this takes the form of strategic planning or visioning. This is not a bad thing, but if the process is used to take the focus off the church's own functioning and onto this new, quick fix, it will fail and only perpetuate the chronic anxiety. This is especially true when an outside consultant is used. The very nature of the relationship will encourage church members to feel hopeful that the consultant has all the answers. Unless the consultant can challenge them to take responsibility for themselves and their functioning, the process is doomed.

Another example is the pastoral change. When things aren't going well in a congregation, one manifestation of the quick fix mentality is to seek a pastoral change.

Here are three examples.

One is when the pastor has no clue about self-defining. She is a "consensus" leader. She wants everybody to get along. She is unable to self-define. This is the epitome of adaptive reactivity. Anxious congregations chew up and spit out this type of leader, and the pastor usually leaves without a fight.

Another example is when the pastor is reactive. She gets defensive. She may even start blaming others. This is classic reactive behavior. The conflict will escalate until she finally gives in.

Finally, a congregation may seek a pastoral change when a leader self-defines and encourages church members to reflect on their own response to challenge. Chronically anxious churches hate this. They start acting up. Anxious blaming toward any number of issues, but especially the pastor, becomes the order of the day. If the pastor is not a self-differentiated leader, then she is likely to get defensive and reactive. This feeds the reactivity of the church. It doesn't take long before church members start saying, "We need a new pastor." This is the quick fix approach. They believe getting a new pastor will take care of everything. By this point, the current pastor is so tired of the drama that she is ready to go. Ironically, if she understood leadership through self-differentiation, she would know that remaining self-defined, while staying emotionally connected to the resistors, is the path to long-term health for the congregation. The problem is that anxious congregations can't withstand the acute, but short-term, pain that is necessary for change and growth. This book is intended to help YOU stay non-anxious, but emotionally connected, through this process.

Lack of Well-Differentiated Leadership

The lack of well-differentiated leadership is not only a symptom of a chronically anxious system; it also contributes to the other four symptoms. Anxious systems make it difficult to be self-differentiated because they create surrounding togetherness pressures. Conversely, poorly differentiated leaders will perpetuate the system's reactivity, herding, blame displacement and desire for a quick fix. Let's unpack well-differentiated leadership to understand how this works.

I use the term non-anxious leadership synonymously with well-differentiated leadership. The term doesn't fully explain the depth of self-differentiation, but it captures the essence of what it looks like. The non-anxious leader is able to maintain her identity in the midst of the surrounding emotional processes. This is not detachment. It is understanding what is going on in the system and not getting sucked into the dysfunction. She is able to do this while staying emotionally connected. Further, the non-anxious leader has clarity of vision and values and can articulate these, even as it makes her vulnerable to attack by others. Most importantly the non-anxious leader is able to persist in a non-reactive way when others in the system work to sabotage her efforts.

Whenever a leader tries to self-define in a chronically anxious system there will be sabotage. This is not conscious. It is a natural reaction to maintain the homeostasis of the system. Homeostasis is "a relatively stable state of equilibrium or a tendency toward such a state between the different but interdependent elements or groups of elements of an organism, population, or group."[5] In any system, whether family, church or organization, the unwritten code of conduct governs how people should act. In anxious systems, this is what creates the surrounding togetherness pressures. When someone violates the code, the system works to maintain the status quo by undermining, pushing out or shutting down the dissenting voice. This is homeostasis. Anxious people don't even realize they are doing it. The characteristics of a chronically anxious system manifest themselves to bring the leader back in line. This is sabotage.

Here is an example of how sabotage works. The pastor of a church has a vision to start a new worship service with more contemporary music. There are two services currently, one at 8 a.m. and one at 11 a.m. She believes a service in the fellowship hall at 9:30 a.m., which is during the Sunday School hour, would be perfect. It would not interfere with the other two services by disrupting their schedule or space in the sanctuary. Further, it would likely reach families who would like to attend worship while their kids are in Sunday School. The logic is perfect. Except chronically anxious systems don't function according to logic. The pastor rallies enough support to get the proposal approved by the church council. That's when the sabotage starts.

Reactivity can be hostile words and attitudes regarding the proposal, but that's usually not the case. It more often comes in the form of hostility about something else. Criticism of the pastor's preaching is often at the top of the list, but it can be any issue. Let's say in this example the focus of the reactivity is the budget, another easy target. Suddenly, people are up in arms about the projected shortfall this year, even though they passed the budget two months prior with no reaction. One highly anxious leader proposes to cut all missions giving, which would amount to a 10% cut that would balance the budget -- a quick fix.

Another anxious member responds that if the denomination would just stop asking for so much financial support things would be fine -- blame displacement. Another member says hopefully that if everyone just pitches in on the spring bazaar, a major fundraiser, they could cover the shortfall -- herding.

None of these responses has anything to do with the pastor's proposal. That's how anxious people in anxious systems work. Conversely, well-differentiated people self-define by articulating what they believe about the proposal. They feel comfortable if others disagree with them. They put the mission of the church first and do not so much seek consensus, but rather the best possible path forward. A leader can work with that.

Anxious systems spew forth their anxiety in ways that provoke crises that a less differentiated leader feels compelled to address. Once they get sucked into defending positions or appeasing those who are upset, they are only perpetuating the system's chronic anxiety. Self-differentiated leaders know better. They are able to stay true to their goals and values amidst surrounding togetherness pressures. It doesn't mean they don't listen or can't change their minds. It does mean that they don't get sidetracked by red herrings that are a means of sabotage. And they realize that the most important thing they can do is function as a non-anxious presence, especially during sabotage. This will be explained more fully, but for now it's helpful to understand how chronically anxious systems work.

Remember that Bowen says the best we can hope for is to function at 70% self-differentiation. This is important because it helps us understand why poorly differentiated leaders can make even relatively healthy systems anxious. The poorly differentiated leader creates anxiety through her inability to take emotional stands. That is, the inability to say, "This is what I believe. This is where I think we should go," as well as the inability to allow others the emotional space to say what they believe without getting defensive. People, in general, and systems, in particular, need well-defined leadership and direction. People want to be led. When a leader is unable to do this in a non-anxious way, it heightens the anxiety in the system. A poorly differentiated leader may do this in one of two ways.

First, she might be a "consensus" leader. She wants everyone to get along and everyone to agree before moving forward. People in a healthy system might see this as reasonable and go along. But, over time, people will start to feel more anxious about expressing their opinions and taking emotional stands. Why? Because everyone needs to agree. Think surrounding togetherness pressures. Even people who had previously felt comfortable with expressing their opinions start to clam up. If the cycle persists, the system will regress to the point that it starts to manifest the characteristics of an anxious church detailed in this chapter.

Second, she might be a "command and control" leader. "Here's where we're going, and YOU need to follow." Her efforts will be focused on convincing others of the "rightness" of her position. This is not an emotional stand. It is less about taking responsibility for her own condition and more about trying to change the minds of others. If someone else disagrees, even in a non-anxious way, she will get defensive, heightening the anxiety in the system. The difference between her and a non-anxious leader is that there is no emotional space for other opinions. Healthy emotional space is created when we self-define, stay emotionally connected and give others the freedom to disagree. The problem with the leader described here is that she can self-define, but she is not emotionally connected and does not give others the freedom to disagree. The results will be the same as the consensus leader. The system will show the symptoms of an anxious church (or family or organization).

Over time, even reasonably healthy people will start to dys-function, as they will have no other outlet for their anxiety. Or they will just leave.

It's also possible for the poorly defined leader to be both. To be blown back in forth between the two extremes because she does not look inward enough to find her own emotion-al resources. She's always looking externally to guide her functioning, increasing her own anxiety and the anxiety of the system. In any of these cases, if the poorly defined leader is the pastor, it can lead the church in the direction of chronic anxiety. Unless there is a highly differentiated layperson who can maintain her own functioning in the midst of the increasing anxiety, it is likely the church will exhibit the characteristics of an anxious system.

This last point is essential to understand. A leader is not necessarily someone at the top or someone who tells others what to do. Even in the corporate world, people are "vol-unteers." Yes, they get paid to do their jobs, but without good leadership they are unlikely to do it to the best of their ability. This is even more true in the church, where relatively few leaders are actually paid staff. In any system, if there is someone who can maintain principled, non-anx-ious stands, while staying connected emotionally, they are leading through self-differentiation. And one non-anxious leader can make a difference.

The rest of this book will show you how you can be that leader.

Chapter 5
The Importance of Vision

"Cat: Where are you going?
Alice: Which way should I go?
Cat: That depends on where you are going.
Alice: I don't know.
Cat: Then it doesn't matter which way you go."

Lewis Carroll, *Alice in Wonderland*

What's your vision? For your life and for the ministry you are serving? Asking this is the same as asking, "Where you are going?"

One of Stephen Covey's "7 Habits of Highly Effective People" is to begin with the end in mind.[1] It not only gives you an idea about where you are going, it also can help you determine which way you should go. A leader without vision is like the character Alice from *Alice in Wonderland*. It won't really matter what you are trying to do, because you don't really know where are you going.

Why Vision Matters

When I speak of vision, I am not talking about a group process where everybody gets together to come up with a rambling statement that gets hung on the wall just so everybody can ignore it. Sarcasm aside, I do believe an organizational statement of mission, vision and values is important. It can create energy, enthusiasm and direction. I've been through this process three notable times, once as a pastor and twice as an executive director. In each case, it helped me as a leader and created clarity for the rest of the body. So this kind of vision is important.

As a Christian, I believe my role as a leader is not to come up with my own vision, but to discern God's vision. This applies to my family, to my volunteer work, to my personal goals and to the ministry I serve. For me, this doesn't happen without prayer, meditation and an understanding of scripture. I spend a lot of time in the future. But it is time seeking God's leading and direction.

The reason the leader's vision is important is that people look to the leader for direction, even if they don't agree with her. From a family systems perspective, the most important thing about a leader's vision is not that it is correct, but that the leader expresses what she believes about the future of the family, church or organization. They don't have to agree -- especially if she can create the healthy emotional space necessary for honest conversation. What she says about the future might make them anxious. But if she has no vision, they will be even more anxious. Nature abhors a vacuum, and the lack of vision is a leadership vacuum that gets filled with the five characteristics of a chronically anxious system.

Vision helps people to imagine a future or preferred reality. It is not a plan. Rather, it is a way for the leader to express her values as they apply to the future. As Simon Sinek said in his "How great leaders inspire action" TED Talk: "Martin Luther King did not give an 'I have a plan speech.' He gave an 'I Have a Dream' speech."[2] Dr. King's speech was all about his own values of equality as they applied to a very big organization -- America. A leader's vision is about self-definition. It is the ability to say, "I believe," while staying connected emotionally to those being led. It is essential to leadership in any organization, especially the chronically anxious church.

Vision as Self-Definition

The key to leadership in an anxious church is self-differentiation. It is the ability to define one's own goals and values amidst surrounding togetherness pressures AND to stay emotionally connected. Self-definition is the component of self-differentiation that is the defining of goals and values. We will get to how to deal with togetherness pressures and how to stay connected later. For now, the key leadership point is this -- if you don't have vision, it's hard to self-define.

From a family systems standpoint, vision is not so much about direction as it is about self-differentiation. A non-anxious leader articulates her vision while giving others the freedom to disagree. When you do this, you are saying, "This is what I believe. This is where I think we should be going. This is how this direction reflects my values." Whether you are right or you are way off base, by defining your own goals and values and sharing them you are on the path to leading through self-differentiation. That's why vision matters. Without it, you will, by default, be promoting anxiety in the system. A family, church or organization hates a leadership void, and a lack of vision creates that void, increasing anxiety.

Two concepts help us to understand how vision as self-definition works. The first, which has already been mentioned, is emotional space. The second is sabotage.

If you articulate your vision in a non-anxious way, you create emotional space that encourages others to self-define. This is not about convincing others that you are right. In all things as a leader, if you are able to say, "This is what I believe. You are free to believe otherwise," you create the emotional space that gives others the opportunity to agree or disagree. Those who are more emotionally mature, that is, self-differentiated, will take that opportunity. They will say something like, "I can see how you might say that, but I disagree because..." or, "I'm on board with you, but I wonder about..." The point is not so much what they say (content), but how they say it (process). They are articulating their own beliefs (self-defining).

The less emotionally mature will respond by trying to define you. They will respond with, "How can you say that? What makes you think that? You just don't understand." Their comments avoid how they feel and focus on what's wrong with you. Even if they agree with you, they will tend not to self-define. "You are such a woman of God. We are so lucky to have you." Those statements may sound nice, but they are not self-differentiated.

Friedman emphasizes this point by saying that if you want to find out who is well-differentiated in a congregation, then preach a sermon on a controversial subject.[3] Make sure to self-define, by sticking with "I" statements such as "I believe," "I feel," and, the most provocative, "I encourage you to think about your own stance on this." After the service, the well-differentiated members of the congregation will define themselves. The less differentiated members will define you. The topic is not important. As we'll see in the next chapter, it's the process, not the content, that matters. If you don't have the opportunity to preach very often, you can do this in a church council meeting or other large group setting. Take a stand and pay attention to the reactions.

As mentioned in the last chapter, sabotage is what often results when you self-define in a non-anxious way. It's almost guaranteed to happen in a chronically anxious church. But even in a reasonably healthy church, there are usually people who are poorly differentiated. And they will push back. Maybe not directly, and maybe not knowingly. They will truly believe that they are doing the right thing. But their efforts, usually focused on something other than the leader's vision, are a result of their own anxiety resulting from the leader's self-definition. If you, as a leader, are experiencing sabotage, then you are on the right track. You have defined your own goals and values and cast your own vision, while giving others the freedom to disagree. Anxious people can't handle this, and the result is sabotage. Leading through self-differentiation not only precipitates this, but it is also the means by which the leader helps the entire system, including those responsible for the sabotage, to move forward with the best possible outcome. This book is about how to do this. For now, it's enough to understand sabotage is the system's natural response when a leader articulates her vision.

A Few More Thoughts about Vision

The more responsibility you have for leading an organization, the more time you need to spend in the future. Not like Marty McFly in *Back to the Future*, but in your mind. It goes back to *Alice in Wonderland*. If you don't know where you're going, it doesn't much matter where you go. Somebody has to be thinking about the direction of the family, church or organization. If you are the leader, a parent, a pastor, an executive director or a CEO, then this is your primary function. Where are you going, and how will you get there? This is vision.

Even if you are not the primary leader, you can apply this to your area of responsibility. Whatever you're leading, whether a committee, a classroom or a department, it's your responsibility to envision a preferred future, how it fits into the mission and purpose of the larger entity and how you will get there.

As I mentioned, when you articulate vision, you don't know for sure if you are right about what you believe. That's why creating emotional space is important. If it is truly God's vision, then the Holy Spirit will be moving on others as well. I have learned that even before "going public" with my thoughts, I will have individual conversations with people who I believe are spiritually mature, as well as focused on God's priorities rather than their own. I will say, "I believe God is leading us to..." My experience has shown me that if it is really God's vision, then at least some people will say, "You know, I think you may be on to something." Or, better yet, "I've been sensing the same leading from God myself." If it's God's vision, eventually a critical mass of people develops who can help move things forward. That's just my experience -- your mileage may vary.

Finally, while I often discern where I believe God is leading, I have never been able to envision the entire path to get there. I believe that's how God works. If God revealed the whole path, that wouldn't be faith. When God asked Abraham to leave his homeland, God didn't tell him where he was going. God just said, "Go."

My own experience with vision is that I get an idea of how the end result might look. And I get an idea of what the first step should be. But the rest is fuzzy. If I had waited for the entire path to be revealed, I never would have gotten started. Faith is asking God to reveal one step, and then taking that step. Then asking God to reveal the next step. It's about moving step-by-step, without knowing the entire path. It's about trusting in the process and focusing on the progress. That is what it means to be a leader.

Being a leader also means dealing with stress. The next chapter shows that self-differentiation is the best approach to handling stress.

Chapter 6
Dealing with Stress

"Life is difficult. This is a great truth, one of the greatest truths. It is a great truth because once we truly see this truth, we transcend it. Once we truly know that life is difficult -- once we truly understand and accept it -- then life is no longer difficult. Because once it is accepted, the fact that life is difficult no longer matters."

M. Scott Peck, *The Road Less Traveled:*
A New Psychology of Love,
Traditional Values, and Spiritual Growth

The Inevitability of Stress

I like to paraphrase Scott Peck this way. Life is hard. The sooner we realize this, the easier it gets.

Stress in life is inevitable. Life is difficult. Our own response to the challenges in life is the biggest factor in whether stress will bury us or invigorate us. Distress is defined as "extreme anxiety, sorrow or pain."[1] Distress buries us. We feel less capable, less able to cope. We feel helpless. In this state, stress is a big problem. However, "eustress" is defined as "a positive form of stress having a beneficial effect on health, motivation, performance and emotional well-being."[2] Eustress gets us enthused about life.

The difference between distress and eustress is the difference between a problem and a challenge. In fact, there is no biochemical difference in your brain between anxiety and excitement. Both are considered emotional states of arousal and are driven by the release of brain chemicals including norepinephrine, cortisol and adrenaline. The difference comes in how we process the situation. If we interpret it as a problem, it results in anxiety and stress. If we interpret it as a challenge, it results in energy and excitement. For example, when speaking in front of an audience, the physical signs of anxiety and excitement are the same. You can interpret it as a problem and be filled with anxiety, or you can interpret it as a challenge and growth opportunity. Challenge is the path to growth. Nobody gets the problem they can handle.

Yes… life is difficult. You can face horrific challenges caused by disease, violence, natural disaster and oppression, just to name a few. But you still have a choice as to how you respond. Victor Frankl survived the Nazi concentration camp in Auschwitz. In his book *Man's Search for Meaning*, he documents his experience and what he observed was the most critical element in survival. It was the response of the individual. He wrote, "When we are no longer able to change a situation, we are challenged to change ourselves."[3] Auschwitz most certainly was a place where one could think that changing the situation was impossible. What Frankl found was that those who had purpose and hope had the best chance for survival. They were able to identify a purpose in life and imagine a positive future to live for. They had vision. Even in this situation of distress, some were able to experience it as "eustress." "Everything can be taken from a man but one thing: the last of the human freedoms -- to choose one's attitude in any given set of circumstances, to choose one's own way."[4]

Fortunately, very few of us will ever face a situation like Auschwitz. But it puts our own stress in perspective. Frankl helps us to understand how important our own response is to defining a situation as a challenge or a problem. We can apply this to any situation.

But what about leadership? There is a very specific type of stress that results from the demands of leadership. These demands often result in burnout, especially for clergy. As with stress, in general, we can identify the key factor in whether a leader will experience eustress or distress. That factor is self-differentiation.

Self-Differentiation Reduces Stress

Friedman writes: "Trying to be creative and imaginative is stressful, being responsible is stressful, maintaining vision is stressful, being on the lookout for and trying to deal with sabotage is stressful. Yet all leaders move in that direction, and not all leaders experience burnout."[5]

There is a basic question you can ask yourself as a leader: "For whom am I taking responsibility?" To the extent that you are taking responsibility for the emotional functioning of others, you will experience distress. This is especially true when you are in a triangle and are taking responsibility for the relationship of the other two, whether they are two people or a person and her issue. When this happens, you can feel stuck and stressed. In Chapter 3, I emphasized that you can't change a relationship to which you do not belong. This is essential to understanding and dealing with emotional triangles. Taking responsibility for the relationship of the other two parts of a triangle will cause YOU to bear the stress of their relationship.

There are two ways you can take responsibility for another. The first is to overfunction. If you're dealing with two people, you try to smooth it over. You work to help them get along better and act as referee. If you're dealing with a person and her issue, you enable her behavior and/or rush in to help her avoid the consequence of her actions. Either way, YOU will be stressed. The second is to get defensive. In this case, you become the focus of anger or blame as a way to stabilize the relationship of the other two. Trying to argue otherwise will only harden their position. The issue is irrelevant because it's the process, not the content, that matters. The process is how others avoid taking responsibility for their own functioning and how you end up with the stress of their relationship, either through overfunctioning or defensiveness.

Friedman challenges the perspective that burnout comes from working too hard, because many, many leaders work hard and don't burn out. So what makes the difference? Leadership through self-differentiation, where your primary focus is taking responsibility for your own emotional functioning. This is much less stressful than taking responsibility for the functioning of others. And this goes back to an understanding of emotional triangles. The main reason a triangle occurs in the first place is that someone is avoiding taking responsibility for her own functioning. And, as mentioned, if you are the third component of the triangle, the stabilizing force, you will either be drawn to overfunction or you will be blamed. In either scenario, if you take the bait, you not only encourage the others NOT to change, but you also will take on the stress of their relationship.

On the other hand, if you focus on defining your own position in a non-anxious but connected way, you are giving back responsibility for their functioning. This will cause them to feel the stress of their relationship and will, at least initially, result in sabotage to bait you back into the triangle. This is when you will feel the most anxiety.

Here are some examples of sabotage:

> Two people are in conflict. When you self-differentiate, their conflict escalates and their intensity to get you to "fix" the other increases.

> A relative has an addiction. When you stop enabling her behavior, her symptoms worsen.

Two people blame you for a problem in the church. When you self-define without getting defensive, the blame escalates.

Your sibling is pressuring you to overfunction with your mother. When you self-differentiate, withstanding the forces for togetherness, her anxiety increases and her pressure on you increases.

Friedman uses the term "the leverage of the dependent" to describe the forces that are at work. Those who do not take responsibility for their own functioning are, by definition, emotionally dependent. Their primary means of avoidance is the emotional triangle. If you are the focus of a triangle, either through baiting to overfunction or blaming for the condition of others, then you are experiencing the leverage of the dependent. The question is, how will you respond?

Self-differentiation is not a ninja mind trick. However, it does reverse the forces at work. When you self-differentiate, it turns those forces back on the dependent. Think of it this way: When you are differentiating, you are focused on defining yourself. The dependent are focusing on defining you, as well. If you defend yourself, if you try to convince them that they are wrong, you will lose. They become an immovable object, and you will feel stressed. However, if you stay focused on what you believe and where you are headed, you don't give the dependent the fight they are looking for. Now, instead of you trying to change them, THEY have to try to change you.

So it comes down to this: What is more stressful, trying to change others? Or withstanding the pressure of others trying to change you? When you take the bait of an emotional triangle, you are trying to change others. You will either overfunction in their relationship, or you will try to convince them that they are wrong in blaming you. This is much more stressful than maintaining a non-anxious presence in the midst of sabotage. The latter is not easy, but it won't bury you emotionally. And the more you do your own work, the easier it will become to self-differentiate in the midst of sabotage.

The most difficult part of this is to self-define AND to stay in touch emotionally. When anxiety increases, you will tend to do one, but not the other. You might take an emotional stand, but you will become rigid and disconnect emotionally. This is narcissism, not self-differentiation. Or you might take the bait. You stay connected emotionally, but you succumb to the surrounding togetherness pressures. In either case, your own input into the system will contribute to the system remaining stuck, not to helping it to find a way forward.

The only way forward is when you can stick to your principles without disconnecting emotionally. The family systems theory of sabotage predicts that things will get worse before they get better. Dysfunction and anxiety will increase before they decrease. Ultimately, leadership through self-differentiation creates the emotional space that dissipates, not intensifies, anxiety -- both your own and that of others. Your capacity to lead in this way has everything to do with how well you function in your own family of origin. If you are unable to take an emotional stand, while maintaining a non-anxious presence in your family of origin, you likely will not be able to do it anywhere else.

I will say it again: This is why doing your own work is so important. Leadership through self-differentiation is not a set of techniques to manipulate conditions and circumstances. It is your presence, non-anxious and emotionally connected, that makes the difference. As we go through the next few chapters, it will be important to remember this. As we discuss how to manage yourself as a leader, apply it first to your own family of origin. Doing this will help you move toward better functioning everywhere, including as a leader.

Chapter 7
Sabotage and the Moment of Truth

Two Types of Crises

As a leader, you will face two types of crises. The first has little to do with your own emotional functioning. It could be an untimely death in the church, a physical event like a natural disaster or a fire, or a change in the local zoning ordinance that requires a significant renovation. In these cases, the challenge is not sabotage -- the challenge is how to work through the issues at hand to survive, and even thrive. It's always good to be a non-anxious presence and self-define, especially in times of crisis. People appreciate and respond to a calm, decisive leader. But these types of crises are rare.

The vast majority of crises that you will face as a leader are your fault, in a good way. That is, to the extent that you are leading through self-differentiation, you will pre-cipitate crises in the system that you are leading. Ironically, this form of crisis, called sabotage, is not due to your failures or inability to lead effectively. It is precisely because you are leading through self-differentiation. The more poorly self-differentiated the system is, in general, the more sabotage you will experience.

It's important to understand that most sabotage is mindless. It is a function of those who are less self-differentiated responding to a change in the homeostasis of the system. It is unwitting pushback against change. It comes less from the actual issue at hand and more from their own unresolved issues in their family of origin and/or the church system. The question is: Will you be prepared for sabotage or surprised by it? To effectively lead change, you must be able to anticipate and prepare for this kind of crisis. Convincing your church to do something new is not even half the battle. It can be hard, but it is possible. However, managing the sabotage that comes next is where most leaders fail.

The Inevitability of Sabotage

Dealing with sabotage is overlooked in most leadership theories. We've been taught that if we are good leaders, then people will be inspired to follow. This is partly true. But what's missing is the inevitability of sabotage. This is especially true when you are leading through self-differentiation. When you take a well-defined, principled stand as a leader, it is almost certain to trigger reactivity by the least self-differentiated.

Rather than seeing sabotage as a reaction to effective leadership, it is better to think of it as a part of the leadership process. Thinking in this way will help to avoid being blindsided by sabotage. When you are leading a change effort, the change itself is only half the process. Once the change has occurred, you need to be prepared for the reactivity that will follow. When you are going to cross the road, getting to the curb is only the beginning -- you better be looking both ways before you start walking across. That's what change is like. The change itself is like getting to the curb. Dealing with sabotage is actually crossing the road. Most leaders get run over on the way or get so scared by the traffic that they retreat from the road. It is only by crossing the road -- that is, effectively dealing with the sabotage -- that you can be assured that the change you are leading is a success.

It's process, not content.

The process is triggered by the change itself. It doesn't matter whether it's a new worship service, a new outreach ministry, a change in staff configuration or a new Sunday School curriculum. It is the change that precipitates the resistance. If you, as the leader, are self-defined and emotionally connected, it will make those who are less so uncomfortable. By definition, they will not deal with their discomfort directly, but will do so by attacking you (blame displacement) or being passive aggressive (baiting you to take responsibility for their discomfort). The better differentiated members of the system may disagree with you, but they will let you know without demanding that you change. In fact, it is likely to be those who "agree" with you that will cause the resistance. They will attack you for something other than the change at hand, or they will cause dysfunction somewhere else in the system, even as they smile at you and say how great the change is. Again, this is most often unwitting. But it is how people deal with their discomfort.

If you understand sabotage as a systemic reaction to leading through self-differentiation, you will be better prepared for it. Just as you are trained to look both ways before you cross the road, you can learn to instinctively look for the reactivity in the system when leading change.

Understanding the systemic nature of sabotage will also make you less likely to take it personally. Because this is a process phenomenon, it has nothing to do with the worthiness of the change or your effectiveness as a leader. In fact, your efforts are being sabotaged BECAUSE of your effectiveness as a leader. When I am coaching a leader and she is experiencing sabotage, I remind her that she is doing something right, which is the opposite of how she feels.

But being prepared for and recognizing sabotage is only one step in the process. The most important part is the moment of truth.

The Moment of Truth

The moment of truth is when most leaders experience failure. Instead of maintaining a principled stand while staying emotionally connected, the leader does only one of the two, or even worse, does neither. Let's break it down.

One failure is for the leader to maintain her stand, but to withdraw emotionally. Unless a leader is able maintain her position AND stay emotionally connected, she will face problems. When a leader is self-defined, but not connected, it heightens anxiety and the symptoms in the system. Because there is no emotional connection, the anxiety from the system's shakeup has no outlet except through greater and greater dysfunction. Narcissistic leaders may win the day temporarily, but they are sowing the seed for mutually assured destruction. Maintaining an emotional connection is key for leaders.

I would also contend that empathy is a good thing, because it helps you to understand where the other person is coming from. Using a systems perspective, you realize that someone is upset, and it is not always because of the issue at hand, but because of unresolved issues in her own family of origin. That's real empathy. It can reduce your anxiety because you won't take things personally, and it will help you stay connected emotionally.

One of the hardest things to do is say, "This is what I believe. I know it upsets you, and I'm sorry. I care for you, *but I'm not responsible for how you feel.*" It's probably best to leave the italicized phrase in your head. But you need to tell yourself that, so you won't give in, even as you stay connected. Leaders who just say, "This is what I believe," without showing care for those who are upset are missing the point of leadership through self-differentiation.

Another failure is to put emotional connection above self-definition. It is giving in. When a leader does this, she is folding her cards amidst the surrounding togetherness pressures. Rather than maintaining her principles and staying connected, she opts for staying connected. This is the "peace at all costs" leader. This type of leader gives all the power in the system to the most emotionally dependent. Those who are least willing to take responsibility for their own emotions vent their anxiety when there is any change in the system, and, because the leader gives in, the system snaps back into place. After a while, she will just give up trying to change things, because it's not worth the emotional upset. This is the leverage of the dependent discussed in the last chapter.

The worst failure of nerve is to give in AND withdraw. This is most likely to occur when the leader has been completely broken by the leverage of the dependent. Either she has tried the narcissistic approach until there is a final showdown, or she has tried to maintain peace at all costs and has no emotional resources left. To give in and withdraw emotionally is the beginning of the end, if not the end itself, for the leader in any system.

How do you maintain your resolve in the moment of truth? I've said this before -- it starts with doing your own work. The more you work to deal with your unresolved issues in your own family of origin, the more likely you will be able to maintain self-differentiation in the moment of truth. Whenever you are feeling anxious, ask yourself: "From where does this come? Where in my own system is this feeling most familiar? How can I rewrite the script so that I'm no longer captive to this feeling?" This is a lifelong process, but the more you lean into and work through your anxiety, the better you will function as a self-differentiated leader.

That being said, there are some things you can keep in mind to help you in the moment of truth.

1. Don't let the crisis at hand consume your world. Maintain your emotional functioning as a whole person, both in the system and outside of it. Not every interaction in the system has to be about the crisis. Let the crisis be what it is: one thing, but not the entire thing. Continue with your activities outside of the system, whether professional or social. Focus especially on the things you enjoy. Not letting the crisis become the center of your universe will better equip you to deal with it when it does come up.

2. Continue to connect with your friends and family without allowing your own anxiety about the crisis to infiltrate everything that happens. Share with them so they can support you, but don't drag them down by allowing it to be the only thing you ever talk about.

3. Focus on your long-term goals. This will keep the situation at hand in perspective. As the saying goes, "It always looks like failure in the middle." Keeping the long view helps you to understand that this is just one more bump in the road.

4. Try to keep things loose. Use humor and playfulness to help others be less serious. Anxiety is poison, and humor reduces anxiety.

Finally, keep the balance between maintaining your stand and being narcissistic. Just because you believe you are right, doesn't mean you shouldn't listen to what others think or pay attention to how others feel. Just because you do so, doesn't mean you have to give in. The moment of truth is about being firm, but fair. Principled, but caring. Differentiated, but connected. It is the hardest thing to do. But it is the only path to lasting change.

Chapter 8
The Necessity for Self-Regulation

Leading through self-differentiation is a balancing act. You have to be willing to take a stand. But you can't disconnect emotionally. You have to show empathy. But you don't want to promote weakness in others. You have to build community and teamwork. But you don't want the forces for togetherness to overwhelm self-differentiation -- in yourself and in others. The good news is you can improve your capacity to do this. The challenge is to find the right balance. To do this, you need to understand that leadership through self-differentiation is a way of being, not a technique.

The Yeager Heresy

In his article "Misreading Family Systems Theory", Leander Harding describes what is known as the Yeager Theory in family systems. He writes:

"Friedman uses the metaphor of General Chuck Yeager and the sound barrier. When the sound barrier was being approached the aircraft would experience more and more turbulence as the plane closed in on the critical speed. Pilots would drive their aircraft to what they thought was the limit and then, afraid that the airplane would shake apart, back off without breaking the barrier. Yeager believed a physicist

friend that it would be smooth on the other side of the barrier and put on speed just when most pilots were backing off
and became the first to break the sound barrier."[1]

Yeager was correct. He had the courage to increase his
speed at the point when the other pilots backed off. Once
he pushed through the sound barrier, he experienced
smooth sailing. Friedman uses the sound barrier metaphor
to describe what one experiences when leading change.
The sabotage comes after change has begun and as things
are beginning to pick up speed. Like pilots before Yeager,
most leaders pull back on the throttle. The turbulence from
the sabotage causes a failure of nerve. Instead of pressing
forward, as a non-anxious presence, the leader gives in to
the sabotage, typically by focusing on the content of the
attacks. As you know, dealing with content, rather than
understanding process, can stop change in its tracks.

Harding maintains that there is a tendency to misinterpret
this metaphor by leaders who lack an understanding of family systems theory, and, more importantly, who do not make
the difficult journey of doing their own work. He coined
the term "Yeager heresy" to describe leaders who are unable or unwilling to discern the difference between taking
a principled stand and becoming rigidly inflexible. Those
who fall for this heresy see the family systems approach as a
"technique" for achieving their goals. They understand the
importance of self-definition and taking emotional stands,
but they miss the important point that they also need to
stay emotionally connected, especially to the resistors.

Leaders who are taught that sabotage and crisis are inevitable when they begin to lead through self-differentiation,
are also taught that they need to avoid getting wrapped up
in content and need to understand the emotional processes
involved. These are all things that I have written in this
book, and Harding does not disagree with them. What he
cautions against is taking a stand in a way that leaves others

no room to do the same thing. When we are a non-anxious presence, we create emotional space where others are also able to self-differentiate. When we see leading through self-differentiation as a technique, we miss the opportunity for real conversation. We are unable to discern between those who are able to self-differentiate and those who are engaging in sabotage. Harding describes it this way:

"They have not heard the challenge that leadership involves staying emotionally connected to the members of the system, especially those with whom they are most emotionally uncomfortable. They have not heard the warning that this leadership theory is primarily about controlling one's own emotionality and not a recipe for handling or manipulating others. The result is a generation of leaders on all sides of the current polarization who think that leadership consists of taking a bold stand and persisting in a damn the torpedoes full steam ahead mode. When resistance arises and the ship threatens to shake apart they are convinced that smooth skies are just ahead and they pour on the speed. They will not be able to perceive that they have not done the personal and relational homework necessary to really make a positive contribution until the wings come off as they now are."[2]

In A Failure of Nerve, Friedman contends that we have allowed a focus on empathy to allow the least mature to hold the rest of us hostage. This is true when we are unable to self-differentiate and when we adapt to those who are making the greatest demands in the system while refusing to take responsibility for themselves. However, I believe that some leaders are misinterpreting Friedman, making themselves susceptible to the Yeager heresy. Empathy, which promotes weakness, maintains anxiety in the system. But empathy combined with a self-defined, non-anxious presence, is leadership through differentiation. Self-regulation helps us to know the difference.

The Conflict of Wills

Self-regulation is controlling your own reactivity to anxious others. When you are faced with sabotage or triangling, you control your need to defend yourself or to lash back with your own anxiety. Likewise, you avoid adaptation. You don't allow anxious others to change your position so you can avoid a confrontation. You remain a non-anxious presence, clearly stating your position, while staying emotionally connected. I may sound like a broken record, but self-regulation is important because it requires intentionality.

You WILL feel anxious. You WILL want to defend yourself or want to withdraw emotionally to avoid conflict. Self-regulation is intentionally controlling these impulses so that you can self-differentiate. The more you have done your own work, the more comfortable you will feel doing this. And, no matter how well-differentiated you become, the higher the emotional stakes, the more anxious you will feel.

The objective of self-regulation is to reduce the conflict of wills. As I noted in the chapter on stress, as long as you are trying to convince others to agree with you, the dependent have the leverage, and you will experience the stress. Trying to convert others also creates a "for or against atmosphere." You are encouraging a conflict of wills. You may be doing this calmly, but as long as your efforts are focused on changing the minds of others, instead of defining your own position, the conflict of wills remains.

At some point in my life, I learned to live by the mantra, "Nobody likes to be told what to do." I'm not saying that, as a leader, you won't have to do this. But it may be far less than you imagine. For example, it's almost always better to ask someone to do something, even if they work for you and you can order them to do it. Telling someone what to do sets up a conflict of wills, even if you have the authority to do so. Likewise, self-differentiating reduces the conflict of wills because you state your own position without trying to convince the other to change her mind. Self-regulating behavior resists the temptation to convert others and focuses on remaining a non-anxious presence.

I once suggested at a staff meeting an idea for a new camp program. Our staff immediately began to state why they thought it was a dumb idea. They didn't actually say "dumb," but that was clearly the message. They weren't calling me dumb either. To their credit, they were stating their own position, clearly defining why they thought the program was not a good idea. I was the one getting anxious. I tried to keep my head and not get defensive. I tried to calmly state why I thought it was a good idea. If I were defensive, I would have focused on the others by defining them. "You don't understand. You are always trying to squash my ideas. You have no idea what is best for this ministry. You better listen, I'm the boss." They create a conflict of wills. Instead, I did my best to remain a non-anxious presence. After about five minutes of vigorous discussion, I tried to lighten the mood. So I turned to one of the staff members who had remained silent and said, "They're all pickin' on me. You haven't said how you feel."

He grinned and said, "There's no need."

We all had a good laugh. And they were right. It was a dumb idea.

Notice that I never told you what my dumb idea was. It's process, not content. The idea was irrelevant. The important element here was what I needed to do to self-regulate to avoid producing a conflict of wills. I advocated for my position in a self-defined way, but I stayed emotionally connected by actually listening to what others were saying. My response was not adaptation; it was listening, then changing my mind. Leadership is sometimes about saying you are wrong.

Feedback and Chronic Conditions

One key to self-regulation is reflection. By pausing and getting distance from any situation, you are better able to observe the emotional processes that are going on in the system. Furthermore, you can prepare yourself to self-regulate, that is, to maintain a non-anxious presence, when the anxiety escalates. To better understand this, you need to understand the nature of chronic conditions and the role of feedback.

Have you ever felt like picking a fight? Not physically, but verbally. Perhaps you had a bad day at the office, and you're mad at your boss. But instead of taking an emotional stand with your boss, you go home, and you pick a fight with your spouse (or sibling, child or roommate; fill in the blank). This is blame displacement. If you've never done this, let me tell you how it goes. You get home and start picking. You lodge some form of complaint against the other, trying to get a reaction. If you are seasoned, you will know exactly which button to push to get the reaction you want. And, voilà! The next thing you know you are yelling and screaming at each other. That feels good, doesn't it?

There is a pattern to this type of pain displacement that is recognizable to most people. If you've been around long enough, you likely have at least one relationship where you can predict exactly how things will go when one person's anxiety gets the process going.

Now, what happens if the other refuses to allow you to push the right button? What if instead of getting defensive and yelling back, she says, "I'm sensing that you had a bad day." She's staying non-anxious and connected. That will make you madder. So you really pour it on and start criticizing to get a reaction. She then says something paradoxical and playful like, "I love when you try to push my buttons. It's such a fun game." Eventually, you will tire of trying to pick a fight and, perhaps, will go deal with your own issues.

This illustrates the principle that when you try to get a re-action out of someone and you don't get it, the energy will dissipate. You'll look elsewhere to dump your anxiety or start taking responsibility for yourself. But, as long as you get the reaction you're looking for, you can displace your anger or pain on the other. That reaction is called feedback.

You'll note two things going on in this example. First, you are triangling the other because you are uncomfortable with your relationship with your boss. Second, as long as you get the reaction you are (subconsciously) looking for, which is the fight, then you can avoid dealing with your own issues between you and your boss. The feedback in this situation is when the other gets defensive or offended or angry and gives you the fight you're looking for. The longer this pat-tern persists, over time, the more likely this condition will become chronic. You will think there is a problem between you and the other, but she is not the problem. You are. The longer you refuse to take responsibility for your own emotional condition, the more chronic the relationship problem between you and the other will become. The most likely way out is for the other to be a non-anxious presence and stop giving you feedback. Then you might decide to take responsibility for yourself and, ultimately, self-differ-entiate with your boss. Or you'll go looking for some other person or issue to triangle.

In a chronically anxious system, there must be feedback to maintain the chronic condition. It functions in a similar manner as described in the example. There is a pattern to how the anxiety flows through the system. The key com-ponent that keeps the system anxious is feedback, either reactive or adaptive. When things start to escalate, the most effective response is to maintain a non-anxious pres-ence, rather than to provide feedback. Things will initial-ly get worse. This is the equivalent of you pressing harder for a fight in the example above. But if you can sustain a non-anxious presence, things ultimately will get better.

To the extent that there is a chronic condition that is perpetuated by reactive or adaptive feedback, you need to look at your own response to work out why it is hard to self-differentiate. The feedback that you provide to perpetuate the anxiety has to do with your ability to self-regulate in your family of origin. For example, if you have trouble self-regulating with your spouse or children, it has more to do with your inability to self-regulate with your own parents or siblings. If you do your own work and learn to take non-anxious, emotional stands in your family of origin, you will increase your ability to be a non-anxious presence in your nuclear family and your church family. In the pattern that characterizes a chronic condition, there are always people who provide the reactive or adaptive feedback to perpetuate it. If this were not the case, the energy would dissipate, and the condition would not be chronic. If you are the one providing the feedback, the reaction has everything to do with the unresolved issues in your own family of origin, not with the provocation itself.

If you are trying to pick a fight with me, and I react, it has more to do with me than you. Otherwise, I could remain calm. Perhaps your tone of voice reminds me of my mother, with whom I could never take a non-anxious stand, so I react by yelling (reactive behavior). Or it reminds me of my father, with whom I could never take a stand, but I adapted by just going along and keeping my resentment inside (adaptive reactivity). My ability to self-regulate will have more to do with how I work through my own issues in my family of origin. If I don't, the dance of anxiety between you and me will become chronic. There may be a lull between incidents, but the pattern will persist.

Why does this matter? In the chronically anxious church (or family or organization), you can begin to recognize the patterns with which anxiety flows, as well as the reactive or adaptive feedback that maintains the energy. You can then look at your own response in these situations to see if you are a source of feedback that keeps the anxiety going or if you are maintaining a non-anxious presence. If you are a source of feedback, then you know you need to work on self-regulation in these situations.

This process applies to both chronic patterns, as just described, as well as to the sabotage that is inevitable when you lead through self-differentiation. In the latter case, there may not necessarily be a pattern, but, as we discussed in the last chapter, you know the sabotage is coming. You can even predict from whom it will come, although you may not always be correct. This is why reflection is so important. The flow of anxiety in a system is hard enough to deal with when you are prepared. It's nearly impossible when it catches you by surprise.

Taking regular time to reflect on the emotional processes in your family, church or organization will help you to see things more clearly. It will help you to anticipate patterns of anxiety in the system and in yourself. It will help you to better self-regulate so that you can exercise integrity in the moment of choice.

Integrity in the Moment of Choice

"Quality of life depends on what happens in the space between stimulus and response."3 (*First Things First*, Stephen R. Covey, Roger A. Merrill and Rebecca R. Merrill)

Integrity in the moment of choice is keeping true to your goals and values when faced with situations, obstacles, challenges and decisions in life. When applied to leadership through self-differentiation, it is remaining a self-defined, non-anxious presence when faced with surrounding togetherness pressures. It is taking a non-anxious, principled stand, even when you are feeling anxious inside. The smaller the gap between stimulus and response, the more likely that you will respond instinctively, according to the hidden code or software that is programmed by your family of origin. More often than not, this type of response is feedback, either reactive or adaptive, that will perpetuate the anxiety of the system.

The more space you have, the easier it is to be true to yourself. Self-regulating is about creating more space between stimulus and response in the moment of choice. It is resisting the urge to respond immediately, even unthinkingly, so you can have time to respond thoughtfully and with intention.

The easiest way to create space is through a technique called anchoring, which includes deep breathing. Anchoring is a form of mindfulness that is counterintuitive. In addition to deep-breathing, you focus on the physical symptoms of your anxiety, as well as your negative emotions. It proves the idea that facing your fear takes away its power. It may feel like you are taking too long to respond, but you should remind yourself that you don't have to respond immediately. It's OK to be thoughtful before you speak.

When faced with a moment of choice that is increasing your anxiety, start breathing deeply. Then focus on your body. Where are you feeling tense? Don't try to change how it feels; just be mindful of the tension, as you continue to breathe deeply. Your body will do the rest. Next, focus on your emotions. What are you feeling? Anxiety, fear, uncertainty, etc.? Don't try to analyze; just be aware. Anchoring will create space for you to act with integrity.

Of course, it may be hard to do this when you have someone in your face. Ideally, you can be paradoxical and playful, lowering the anxiety of the situation and avoiding getting sucked into arguing content. But this is not natural for most of us. It is not a technique. The more you do your own work, the easier it will be to self-differentiate in anxiety producing situations. I will continue to emphasize that this is a life's work that takes intentional, ongoing work within your own family of origin.

With all that being said, there are some techniques that you can use to create space between stimulus and response. These are not about the response itself; they are all about self-regulation. They will help create more room to work on a self-defined, non-anxious response. When faced with an intense, anxiety-filled moment that demands your response, the first thing you must do is to resist the urge to react immediately and instinctively, as this rarely goes well. The best way to self-regulate is to say, "Thank you for sharing." This acknowledges the "stimulus" of the other without getting into the content. It affirms their right to feel the way they do, however dysfunctional or threatening, without validating the logic behind the feeling. Most importantly, it maintains the emotional connection that is critical to maintaining a non-anxious presence.

After saying thank you, you can ask a question. Even if you can't pull off playfulness, you can listen. Listening enables you to be both non-anxious AND emotionally present. The best questions are open-ended questions. These typically include, "Who, What, When, Where and How." You may notice that I omitted "Why." This is because people often have a hard time articulating why they feel what they feel. It can often sidetrack the conversation or even kill it. A good question to ask is, "What makes you feel this way?" Open-ended questions can keep you engaged and non-anxious without arguing content. Using this approach is part of a skill called reflective listening.

The other part is to reflect back what they are feeling. You can say, "I sense that you are...." Fill in the blank -- angry, confused, upset, etc. Again, avoid getting into content, but affirm that you understand how they feel.

Then you need to buy yourself some time. There are a variety of ways that you can respond without responding so you can create emotional space.

"I'm not sure how I feel about this."

"I need some time to think about this."

"I need to pray about this."

If you can string these three responses together in a firm, non-anxious way, you can take command of the situation in a way that maintains an emotional connection, as well as creates space between stimulus and response. This works best when a situation takes you by surprise. But once you have created that space, you still need to respond at some point in a self-differentiated way. Especially if it is a form of sabotage, blame displacement or triangling. You WILL need to take a stand. The next chapter on managing anxiety will show you how.

Chapter 9
Managing Anxiety

God grant me the serenity to accept the things
    I cannot change,
Courage to change the things I can,
And wisdom to know the difference.

The Serenity Prayer by Reinhold Niebuhr
(as adapted for the 12-step movement)

Perhaps the greatest contribution of family systems theory is the wisdom to know that the only thing we can
really change is our own input into the system. Rather than
be overwhelmed by the many things that we can't change,
we can focus on our own behavior, our own functioning.
This is managing self. It is not self-centered or narcissistic.
Done properly it is life-giving to ourselves and the systems
in which we function.

Presence vs. Technique

Leadership through differentiation is not about technique.
While I have shared some techniques that may help in various situations, these are only helpful to the extent that
they are helping you to manage your own anxiety, to limit
your own reactive feedback into the system. You can think
of these as "defensive" measures. They help you to avoid

making mistakes. But if you spend your entire time trying to avoid mistakes, you're unlikely to be a leader people will want to follow.

To achieve this, you need to understand presence. Presence starts with knowing who you are. This is where doing your own work is essential. Understanding your own family of origin and your place in it will not only help you to break the "code" that may drive your reactivity, it can help you to reprogram how you respond in the future. Reflective practices will also serve you well. Prayer, meditation and journaling enable you to pause to think about what really matters to you. More importantly, they invite God into the process to provide clarity and discernment.

But presence is more than just knowing yourself. It's about staying connected emotionally. This is the hardest part -- staying connected, while remaining non-anxious. But this is the power of presence: knowing yourself combined with emotional connection. At this point in your life, you probably realize that true power does not come from position. Even if your position comes with authority, it doesn't mean people will follow. And if they follow, it doesn't mean they will like it and give their best effort. This is true in the family, at work and in the church. There is power in being a non-anxious presence, which is not based in directing, manipulating or cajoling. It is providing true leadership, while giving others the freedom to disagree.

Presence is not only powerful; it is also attractive. There is something about a leader who knows herself that draws people to her. When there is relationship (emotional connection), it is even more powerful. When she gives followers the freedom to follow, or not, in a non-anxious way, it is the most powerful. This is the power of presence. It is rooted in clarity and connection, not in coercion or compulsion.

The problem that most of us face is that this kind of presence makes us extremely vulnerable.

The Power of Vulnerability

> "Vulnerability is the birthplace of innovation creativity and change."[1]

> Brené Brown

If you haven't seen Brené Brown's TEDxHouston talk on the power of vulnerability, it is a well-spent 15 minutes. It is one of the most watched TED Talks ever. Brown shares her own journey from shame to vulnerability and the positive impact that it has had on her life. What was the essential element for her to get from shame to vulnerability, from negative to positive? She did her own work. She went inward and deconstructed the software that prevented her from embracing vulnerability.

Vulnerability is an essential element of leadership through self-differentiation. When you say, "This is what I believe. This is where I think we should go," you are putting yourself out there and becoming vulnerable. You are opening yourself up to attack and criticism. If you do this without staying connected emotionally (narcissism), you are succumbing to the temptation to be invulnerable. Yes, you are self-defining, but you are afraid to engage emotionally, lest you be attacked. This is the problem with the "Yeager heresy" mentioned in the previous chapter. Leadership through self-differentiation is not self-defining, then putting up emotional armor so that you won't be hurt by the inevitable attacks. It is self-defining *and* engaging emotionally, DESPITE the fact that you know you will be attacked. The key to managing anxiety is knowing your own inner workings well enough to not let the attacks bring you down. It is difficult work.

In her book *Daring Greatly: How the Courage to Be Vulnerable Transforms the Way We Live*, Brown puts it this way: "Vulnerability sounds like truth and feels like courage. Truth and courage aren't always comfortable, but they're never weakness."[2] She goes directly at the cultural myth that vulnerability is weakness, contending that it's the opposite. Friedman argues that leaders not only need to learn to embrace vulnerability, they need to learn to *love* it. This indeed takes courage. Friedman and Brown are on the same page, as Brown writes:

"Vulnerability is not weakness, and the uncertainty, risk and emotional exposure we face every day are not optional. Our only choice is a question of engagement. Our willingness to own and engage with our vulnerability determines the depth of our courage and the clarity of our purpose; the level to which we protect ourselves from being vulnerable is a measure of our fear and disconnection."[3]

To be an effective leader, you need to not only learn to choose purpose and connection over fear and disconnection, but you also need to learn to love it, to embrace it.

Author Seth Godin writes in his blog post "*Out on a limb*," that when you are doing important work, you will say to yourself, "This might not work." He writes: "At some level, 'this might not work' is at the heart of all important projects, of everything new and worth doing. And it can paralyze us into inaction..."[4] In this case, he is referring to projects, but this also applies to leadership. It is the essence of choosing adventure over safety. To be a leader implies that you are going somewhere. This, by definition, involves change. And change is scary. What I want you to do is to think of adventure and vulnerability as synonymous. Then learn to embrace them. To love the feeling of putting yourself out there. Why? Because it's the only way to lead positive change. Further, if you can withstand the inevitable sabotage, people will find this kind of vulnerability attractive.

At the heart of managing anxiety in this way is focusing on self-definition and connection without worrying about what people think. This is hard because vulnerability leaves you exposed. You feel open to attacks that can wound you as a person and as a leader. And, understanding sabotage, you know the attacks are likely. Managing self means that you know the attacks are coming, but, because you know who you are and what you believe, they won't really wound you. They may not feel good, but your sense of self is stronger than the attacks. Most importantly, your energy goes into managing who you are, not trying to change the minds of others.

Godin puts it this way:

"Of course, trying to control what other people think is a trap. At the same time that we can be thrilled by the possibility of flying without a net and of blazing a new trail, we have to avoid the temptation to become the audience, to will them into following us. Not only is it exhausting, it's counterproductive. Sales (of concepts, of services, of goods) don't get made because you've spent a sleepless night working on your telekinesis. They happen because you've made something worth buying, because you've outlined something worth believing in.

'This might not work' is either a curse, something that you labor under, or it's a blessing, a chance to fly and do work you never thought possible."[5]

Godin is talking about the sale of one of his book projects. But the same principle applies to leadership, which is, as he writes, the "sale of a concept." He is illustrating a key principle of leadership through differentiation. This makes you vulnerable. You put yourself out there with what you believe, and you think to yourself, "This might not work." That's scary, and you want to do everything possible to make it work. But trying to change other peoples' minds is counterproductive and exhausting. You can only manage yourself. The question is: What do you do with the anxiety that you feel?

When Anxiety Strikes

By now, you should clearly understand that when you are leading through differentiation in an anxious system, you will face sabotage. This is when anxiety strikes. Less differentiated people will blame you, triangle you and attack you, sometimes to your face, sometimes behind your back. Let's be clear: Managing anxiety is not about controlling the anxiety of others. It's about managing your own. Doing so will enable you to maintain a non-anxious presence when others are not. It is this presence that is so powerful. The previous chapter detailed how self-regulation can help you to avoid being reactive to anxious people and anxious systems. But what do you do when YOU are feeling anxious?

Remember that the higher the emotional stakes, the more likely you will feel anxious when others push back. What you do with that anxiety will make you or break you as a leader. If you are unable to self-regulate, your anxiety will take over in ways that will intensify the anxiety in the system. You will either lash out, or you will withdraw. Both have the same result in heightening the anxiety of others. So how do you remain calm, cool and collected? How can you stand firm in your position, while giving others the freedom to have their own? How can you stay connected to others emotionally, even as they are attacking you or withdrawing from you? Let's look at three approaches.

First, do your own work (have you heard this enough?). This is the first and best approach. It takes the longest, so the results are not necessarily immediate. Done properly, it will have the most significant results. It will enable you to work toward being a non-anxious presence naturally. In her TEDx talk, Brené Brown said that when she realized she was going to have to do her own work, she said to herself, "This is going to suck."[6] Doing your own work is not easy. It might be painful. But what is more painful: going through an intense period of self-reflection and exploration, or a lifetime of anxious functioning?

You can do your own work without a counselor or therapist, but working with a professional is more likely to result in a steady path to better functioning. Make sure that the person you see uses a family systems approach. That being said, there are many who do their own work without a professional. If you choose the latter, you need to read *Generation to Generation*, or at least find a group or a class to help you to better understand family systems theory. Regardless of your approach, a genogram and family timeline are essential tools for doing your own work. Chapter 11 will cover these in depth.

When you feel anxious, ask yourself, "Where does that come from in my family of origin?" Remember, anxiety has more to do with your own unresolved relationships in your family system than with anything else. As I mentioned, I realized that much of my conflict avoidance came from my inability to take an emotional stand with my mother. I would not have understood this without doing my genogram. Once you identify which unresolved relationships result in anxiety in your current functioning, you can begin to rework those relationships. This is not about blaming. It is about taking responsibility for your own functioning. You can rework a relationship directly, if the person is alive, or in your mind, if the person is deceased. This is where a counselor, therapist or coach is most helpful. Regardless, it is this process that will free you from the "software" that currently commands your anxiety and reactivity.

The purpose here is not to give you the quick fix, but to give you a hint about the kind of deep work that can truly make a difference in your life. Most people never go there. I hope you will.

All the work you do to self-differentiate will ultimately pay off, if you stick with it. In addition, coaching and/or role-playing can have a significant impact on your ability to lead through self-differentiation. As I have written, there is a pattern to interactions involving chronic anxiety. This can help you to anticipate sabotage, whether in your family, church or organization. Not always, because there will be times when someone vents their anxiety in a way that surprises you. Sometimes it is just a reasonably healthy person who is having a bad day. Other times, it may be someone who normally functions pretty well, but who is going through some type of personal challenge. In these cases, I always ask myself, or the person I'm coaching, "What is going on in this person's family system that is precipitating her anxiety?" You may be caught off guard by the anxiety, but it is a clue that something is going on with her personally. It also becomes an opportunity to provide a caring presence. This is where doing your own work is most helpful. When someone who is not normally difficult to deal with becomes a challenge, you know something has changed. The homeostasis in her family system has gone out of whack. By providing care and concern in a non-anxious way, you can help her to work through this in a way that will not only improve her functioning in her family of origin, but it also will improve her functioning in the church system.

Whether it is a chronic situation or a new challenge, you can help yourself by thinking through your input into the system. In chronic situations, you can pretty well predict how things will go. Go through it in your mind or with someone you trust. Think about what will trigger the anxiety. Think about how it will come out. You likely will know who will react. You can probably even predict the types of statements they will make. More importantly, think about how you can provide a non-anxious response. This is where role-playing is helpful. When I know that I am going to face an anxiety producing situation, I work through the conversation in my mind. When I say anxiety producing, this means both for the person I am facing, as well as myself. Just because I am working toward self-differentiation doesn't mean I don't get anxious. By playing out the conversation in my head in advance, I am helping to de-sensitize myself to my anxiety, as well as the anxiety that is spewed at me.

Here is an example of how working through situations in advance with a coach and/or through role-playing can help. A colleague contacted me about a former pastor who was coming back into the area and doing weddings for members of the congregation. The weddings weren't at the church, and the colleague and his predecessor never had contact. However, some people in the congregation were upset because they felt it was interfering with my colleague's ministry. His dilemma was that those who were close to the former pastor were happy with what was happening. I knew that his only option was to be a non-anxious presence. If he criticized the former pastor, this would be reactive feedback that would intensify the situation and perhaps even make it chronic. We focused on process, not content, and worked through some non-anxious responses to the anxiety of the congregation.

For example, if one of his supporters came and said, "Do you know that the former pastor is doing weddings for church members?" he could respond, "People do love him." Note that this response is non-anxious and doesn't argue content.

Within six months, the problem had gone away.

There are two ways that role-playing the conversation helps you. First, it helps you to manage your own anxiety. By anticipating the situation, you are experiencing the feelings of anxiety, which will better prepare you to handle it effectively. By working through potential responses in advance, you are better prepared to respond to the anxiety as a non-anxious presence. If you can actually role-play your responses out loud with a friend or coach, you will be further ahead. The concept of "fake it till you make it" applies here. When you are actually with the person who is giving you an anxious response, you are likely to feel anxious.

By practicing your non-anxious responses in advance, you can regulate your feedback into the system, even if you are feeling anxious.

This is a good time to emphasize the importance of humor. Used properly, humor helps to keep things looser. It lowers the emotional stakes and the anxiety levels. As I have mentioned, this is only if the humor is not seen as sarcasm. The difference between humor and sarcasm is emotional connection. When you have worked to keep an emotional connection with those who "oppose" you, then humor can loosen things. If you have withdrawn emotionally, humor can make things worse. The idea of keeping things loose is essential in leading through self-differentiation. It is not that you don't take things seriously. It's not that you don't care about the people you are leading. Keeping things loose makes it easier for everyone to function in relationship to you and to one another.

Practicing humor and looseness is difficult. The very act of role-playing tends to make it feel scripted, which is the antithesis of looseness. The latter is supposed to come naturally and feel natural. But if you don't anticipate the situation, if you don't think about non-anxious responses that could help keep things loose, and if you don't practice them in advance, you will have a more difficult time. This is especially true if you are not doing your own work. Even if you ARE doing your own work, this type of preparation is essential to leading through self-differentiation.

Practicing humor and looseness is not unlike the preparation of a stand-up comic. She knows her jokes verbatim. She doesn't leave any word to chance. She practices and practices and practices. Sometimes she'll do this in front of a mirror. Or she'll record it and then play it back to critique timing and tone. By the time she gets up on stage, she is so well-prepared that the words seem to flow naturally. But a better term than naturally is prepared.

This is how role-playing should work when you are leading through self-differentiation. When you can anticipate sabotage and anxiety, you can prepare yourself to be a non-anxious presence. You may feel like you are faking. You may feel uncomfortable in the moment. I still do in some situations. You will probably feel nervous. But, like the stand-up comic who is well-prepared, your audience will think it is coming naturally. And, as a leader who is non-anxious and emotionally connected, you help to bring the anxiety level down for most everyone in the room.

Having someone who can coach you can help tremendously. Someone who understands family process AND who is not tied emotionally to your systems can help you to see things with some distance, which reduces the anxiety of the situation. She can then help you to anticipate anxiety producing situations, work through how they are likely to go down and role-play possible responses with you so you can remain non-anxious and emotionally connected. You can also do this by finding a group of like-minded people who regularly connect to "unpack" situations and who give each other helpful guidance. The key idea here is that you can really benefit from the emotional distance that others have from your situation.

I must emphasize that all this preparation is not to be manipulative. It is to help you manage your own anxiety and your feedback into the system. It's process, not content. By anticipating and role-playing, you are trying to avoid getting pulled down into the content bog. If you argue issues or get defensive when sabotage and anxiety strike, you've already lost the opportunity to lead through self-differentiation. You will never be able to do this if you don't start doing your own work. And I have not met many people who are able to be a non-anxious presence easily in the most intense situations. It takes a lifetime of work for most of us. That is why role-playing and coaching can be so helpful.

This chapter focused on sabotage you can anticipate. When you are caught off guard, the best you can do is to remain non-anxious and not get entangled in content. For this, remember the techniques we covered in the last chapter to deal with the situation and to buy you some time. Once you have time, you can prepare your response and practice it.

Now that we have looked at anxiety in terms of individual interactions so that you can be prepared to be your best non-anxious presence, let's look at your role as a leader in a relationship system.

Chapter 10
Managing the Relationship System

When you are leading through self-differentiation, you have the ability to get some distance from the emotional climate of the systems in which you function. This is more art than science. If you get too much distance, you will disconnect from the system, which brings problems of its own. And, of course, if you have too little distance, you will get sucked into the vortex of anxiety that makes it nearly impossible to function as a non-anxious presence.

The appropriate distance is a balancing act. You must maintain a clear enough head and sense of your own presence to distinguish between process and content in the system. You must self-regulate so that you can avoid providing the anxious feedback that gives dysfunction its energy. Yet you can't remain an aloof, uninterested observer. You must stay connected emotionally to those in the system, especially the most anxious, so that your presence can be a positive force. This will make you vulnerable and uncomfortable.

My own experience is that just having an understanding of family systems theory, as I have laid it out, is a good start. It provides the perspective necessary to get outside your head, so you can be an "observer" of the system. At the same time, it reminds you that you must be more than just an observer. You have to engage emotionally.

Most of what we have discussed thus far has been focused on your own functioning as it relates to the functioning of the system. However, as a leader it is also your job to manage the system itself. This is more than just a series of interactions with individuals, whether they are anxious or not. And it's more than just understanding emotional process. It requires an understanding of how you as a leader can manage and influence the health and direction of the system.

Charisma and Consensus

When you, as a leader, take on the task of managing relationship systems, you need to understand the dual traps of charisma and consensus. Friedman introduces this concept in *Generation to Generation*, in his chapter on Leadership and Self.[1] He contends that most leaders will be somewhere on a continuum between charisma, at one end, and consensus, at the other. The charismatic approach to leadership is personality-based. Followers are drawn to the leader and succumb to her will. Sometimes willingly; other times grudgingly. Either way, it's about the will of the leader. Conversely, the consensus approach is focused on getting followers to agree with each other. It is about their will, not the will of the leader.

Let's look at each to consider why they are traps for the self-differentiated leader.

Since charisma is about personality, it is hard to teach; but it can be cultivated. It makes the most out of a personality that attracts others and can even inspire them. At her best, a charismatic leader can unify different elements within a system. This tends to work best when people in the system are feeling hopeless, helpless and hungry for a change. A charismatic personality can provide hope, even if she is doing it by appealing to the desire for a quick fix.

The problem with charismatic leadership is that it tends to polarize as easily as it can unify. That's because this style of leadership is so focused on the personality of the leader that it's hard for people to separate their emotions from the issues themselves. It also creates an atmosphere of "you are either with us or against us." This not only creates polarization within the system, but also almost always creates a polarization with those outside the system. Cults are the extreme example of systems with a charismatic leader, which helps to explain the biggest problem with charismatic leadership -- it tends to create clones among the followers. This is ironic, since the attraction is the individual personality of the leader.

You should probably get by now that a leadership style that creates clones is antithetical to leadership through self-differentiation. While there is nothing wrong with a leader having charisma, this is not an essential quality of an effective leader. Leadership through self-differentiation is about articulating one's goals and values while giving others the freedom and emotional space to disagree. Because charismatic leadership is so focused on the personality of the leader, disagreeing with the leader is essentially a rebuke of who she is. Those who disagree with one who leads through charisma don't last long in the system. They are either tossed out, or they leave on their own. Even though those who remain may be happy, the system itself is not healthy.

Systems with charismatic leaders can function for a long time, keeping those who agree happy and churning through those who don't. But they will have tremendous difficulty with succession. They will likely feel lost without their leader. They also will have a tendency to "chew up and spit out" any successors, whose biggest sin is that they are not the one who was lost.

Finally, those who lead through charisma are susceptible to burnout or a moral failure. This is because this type of leadership is extremely hard on the leader. Friedman writes: "He or she is perpetually forced to overfunction, most constantly balance all the triangles, and, in the long run, paradoxically finds that his or her functioning has become dependent on having a family to lead. For all these reasons, and more, the charismatic leader remains in a chronic state of stress."[2]

The wonder is not that so many charismatic leaders of churches have burned out or fallen -- it's that so many have not.

At the opposite end of the spectrum from charisma is consensus. Instead of focusing on the personality of the leader, the focus is on the will of group. This approach seeks to minimize conflict and polarization. It values peace, sometimes at all costs. And it values feelings and relationships over ideas. A consensus leader does not share her own goals and values, but instead acts as a facilitator to help identify the will of the group.

As you might imagine, consensus leadership has its own problems. The biggest is that when leading by consensus, a leader and group are always susceptible to being blocked by the most obstinate among them. This can result in a tyranny of the minority. This may seem obvious, but many consensus leaders don't seem to get this. If you are seeking to achieve group consensus before acting as a family, church or organization, it only takes a few holdouts to keep things from moving. If you've ever been in this situation, you know that the holdouts often don't care about what others think or that they are in the way of progress. For whatever reason -- their own fear, anxiety or obstinacy -- they will put you in the position of having to convince them to agree with the rest of the group. A consensus leadership style, combined with the tyranny of the minority, is what sets small churches on the path to death and dying.

Related to this problem is the fact that consensus-led groups tend to lack imagination. By definition, these groups value surrounding togetherness pressures. This discourages individual thought, because any time one comes up with an idea, it has to go through the gauntlet of group evaluation. Collaboration is good, but group-think or a hive mind does not lend itself to innovation, change or courageous thinking.

Another problem is that leaderless groups tend to panic more easily. When things get tough, there is no one to say, "This is what I believe we should do. Here is where we should go." By definition, a consensus-led group tends to be leaderless because the leader is either unwilling or unable to take an emotional stand. If she does, there will be the inevitable pushback and reactivity, because she has disrupted the homeostasis of the group. Finally, consensus-led groups are no less susceptible to polarization or cultic togetherness than groups with a charismatic leader. They get there in a different way: through surrounding togetherness pressures, rather than individual personality. But they can just as easily line up against each other in conflict or have a cultic togetherness where it's "us against the world."

I described leading through charisma or consensus as traps. When you choose to lead on the charisma side of the continuum you are, by definition, separating yourself from those being led. There is you, the leader, who stands apart from the group. And there is the group itself. As you should know by now, this is antithetical to systems thinking generally and family systems thinking in particular. When you choose to lead on the consensus side of the continuum, the opposite problem occurs. You as the leader are no longer a "self." Worse yet, the system has no leader, just a facilitator.

Leading through self-differentiation blows this model up. It refuses to play by these rules. Interestingly, at times it can look like leading through consensus and, at other times, like leading through charisma. There is nothing that says you can't have a personality or try to inspire people. At the same time, there is nothing to say that you can't listen to learn what the majority of people are thinking. But when you lead through self-differentiation, you don't think of either approach as the primary focus of your leadership. The primary focus is to be able to self-define while staying emotionally connected.

To avoid the traps of charisma and consensus, it's important to understand how similar they may look to leading through self-differentiation. A key part of leading through self-differentiation is staying in touch emotionally. Without emotional connection, you, as the "head," are disconnected from the body. You may know where the body should go and may even be able to articulate it, but, if you haven't stayed in touch, the synaptic gaps between you and the body will be too large for your nerve impulses to connect. The danger of emotional connection is that you lose yourself in the body. This is what happens in consensus leadership. The leader is no longer distinguishable from the body. This is the first trap. Staying in touch is NOT the same as leading through consensus.

When leading through self-differentiation, just as important as staying in touch is the ability to self-define. Your ability to say, "This is what I believe, this is what I think we should do, this is where I think we should go," while, at the same time, giving others the emotional space to self-define, is central to leading through self-differentiation. The problem is, it's hard to do this and stay in touch. When you are leading through charisma, you are self-defining, but you are not in touch emotionally. You leave no room for others to disagree. You might think you are being self-defined, but you are really being a narcissist. This is the second trap. It is the Yeager heresy that was described in Chapter 8.

Central to understanding leading through self-differentiation is the concept that followers want to be led. This is why leaderless systems are so anxious: People want to be led, but nobody is doing it. That's why consensus doesn't work. At the same time, people want to be acknowledged as individuals in their own right. They don't want to just be told what to do and asked to follow blindly. That's why charisma often doesn't work. When it does work, through force of personality, it will take its toll on the leader and make it nearly impossible for anyone to succeed her effectively.

When you lead through self-differentiation, the better-differentiated members of the system will respond accordingly by self-defining in a non-anxious way. Those who are taking their own positions are not blindly following, as a charismatic leader would require. Nor are they seeking agreement among all the members of the system. Because the leader has modeled self-differentiation, they are able to do the same. Because the leader has stated her own position in a non-anxious way, while staying in touch emotionally and giving others to the freedom to do the same, the better differentiated persons feel free to take their own positions, whether or not they are in agreement with the leader.

There are two important points to remember here. First, this is all about the position of leadership. Taking a non-anxious, emotionally connected position is independent of personality. Certainly you can be charismatic and do this, but it is not essential. You can be quiet and reserved and still do the same. This would not be charismatic. The important part is that you can communicate a confidence in your own beliefs. This is a what a leader does and what the position requires. Second, when better-differentiated members take their own non-reactive positions, you should feel free to engage and discuss content. "It's process NOT content," doesn't mean you never discuss content. It's being able to understand emotional process well enough to know when it's appropriate. When people are able to define themselves without defining you, and they do it in a non-anxious, connected way, you can feel confident that you will be able to discuss content with them without having to agree. The beauty of this is that the more you lead in this way, the more you will find this taking place. In some systems, this may take years, but over time, if you maintain a non-anxious presence, it will become more and more frequent.

Now, the bad news. Remember that when you take a self-defined, emotionally connected, non-anxious position, this will trigger reactivity among the lesser differentiated persons in the systems. This is sabotage. This is the moment of truth, described in Chapter 7. The sabotage will be characterized by extreme seriousness and will come automatically from those who are poorly differentiated.

I have found that understanding sabotage as an automatic, unthinking response helps me to remain non-anxious and not take things personally. Those who try to sabotage really don't even understand that they are doing this. They aren't doing it because of who I am; they are doing it because of my position as the leader. What keeps me focused is that I know if I can maintain a non-anxious presence, then I am not only giving the whole system a chance to evolve, I am also giving individuals in the system the opportunity to work out their own issues.

You can do this if you can self-define in non-anxious ways, stay in touch emotionally and distinguish process from content. You must do all three to give the system a chance. This is the most challenging part of leadership and the place where most fall short. So, whether you are a pastor or a layperson in a position of leadership, you can make a difference by leading through self-differentiation. It is not easy work, and it requires determination and patience. However, systems can change with this kind of leadership.

Now that you understand the traps of leading by charisma and consensus, it's important to distinguish the difference between togetherness and "stuck-togetherness."

Togetherness vs. Community

Togetherness is a good thing. Anything worth achieving is hard to do alone and is always better when people come together with a common purpose. I think of Christian community as a group of people who have self-identified as followers of Jesus. This can mean many things, so it may vary widely among individuals. People interpret the Bible differently, they worship differently and their understanding of serving God can differ. There will even be a wide variety of understandings of what it means to follow Jesus within the same congregation. Nonetheless, in a Christian community, there is some understanding, however hard it may be to pin down, that it is about Jesus.

But it's clear that in a Christian community not everybody thinks the same, acts the same and believes the same things. When a congregation begins to start thinking and believing all the same things, it is exerting surrounding togetherness pressures that can result in "stuck-togetherness." As we learned in the last section, this can result from charismatic leadership, where people become clones. It can result from consensus leadership, where everyone must agree. In either situation, the pressure to conform is great, and better differentiated members often get frustrated and leave.

What is "stuck-togetherness?" It is the sense that disagreement is negative and those that don't go along are troublemakers. People will rarely express this explicitly, but if you've ever been in a system like this, you know what it feels like. Change is very difficult where togetherness rules.

In contrast, in a Christian community there is a sense of commonality in Jesus, but everyone feels free to work out their own salvation with fear and trembling (Philippians 2:12). There is a maximum of self-definition, even while people are emotionally connected. People feel free to express their own positions, even as they give others the freedom to express their own. Disagreement is not feared, because this is the way to find the best possible path. This may sound like a fantasy world to you, but to me, the goal of any leader should be to move the congregation from togetherness to community. As a leader, it is your job to recognize the difference. How do you do this?

Lead through self-differentiation. When you lead this way, it will automatically result in the better differentiated people self-defining in non-anxious ways. They will follow your lead. Remember: They will not necessarily agree with you, but they will state their positions by defining themselves, without reactivity. The lesser differentiated people will respond by trying to define you, often in very reactive ways. "How can you say that?" "What kind of leader would do that?" "You are taking us down the wrong path." Etc. They may also respond by triangling you. "People are really unhappy about this." Notice that she is not taking responsibility for her own position. She is dealing with her own discomfort by putting the focus on a third leg -- "people." Your job as a leader is to recognize the difference between process and content and to respond accordingly. When people are self-differentiated, it's OK to engage in content, because they are not so much trying to change you as they are expressing their own position. You might even change your mind. Being self-differentiated is not the same as being obstinate.

When people try to define you, especially when their anxiety surfaces (but not always), then there is something going on within them that has nothing to do with you. If you engage in content you are sunk. Your best response is to keep things loose, perhaps even humorous, to not get sucked into a war of words or to try to convince others to agree with you. They will only push back harder. If you remain non-anxious without arguing content, you put them in the position of trying to change your mind. As we discussed in

Chapter 6, it is much less stressful to remain a non-anxious presence and force others to try to change you than it is to try to convince others to agree with you.

When you learn to see the system in this way, it's almost as if you see people walking around with labels on their forehead that only you can see. The labels identify their level of self-differentiation. This is not so you can judge them and condemn those who are not as "evolved" as you. This is so you can understand how to respond in any given situation. More importantly, it helps you to gauge the health of the system. When there are more people who can function in self-differentiated ways, especially in leadership, the system will be healthier. This is true for families, churches and organizations. When the opposite is true, you know that you can expect some tough sledding, because there will be much more reactivity and sabotage. But know this: If you lead through self-differentiation and can maintain a non-anxious presence, over time the system will change. The anxious ones will either deal with their own issues or leave. The non-anxious presences will follow your lead and will help tip the balance. If you are in a chronically anxious church, this could take a good bit of time and a lot of prayer and patience. But you will not only be leading the church to greater health, you will be leading it to greater effectiveness.

Work with the Motivated, Not the Symptomatic

If you are like most people, you will tend to focus your attention on the most symptomatic person in the system, whether it's your family, church or organization. The squeaky wheel gets the grease. This is a natural response. When someone is acting up, causing trouble, spewing anxiety or otherwise demanding attention, you feel like you need to do something about it. Worse yet, others may demand you do something about it. Talk about being triangled.

If you have learned anything about family systems, remember this: Anxious, disruptive, destructive or sabotaging behavior goes beyond the symptomatic person. It is a product of the system itself, as well as other connected relationship systems. This is true whether the symptoms are self-destructive, such as substance abuse, or disruptive, such as sabotage. The likelihood of making significant progress with the symptomatic is low, if not impossible. This is especially true if you are being triangled. If the third leg of the triangle is an issue, such as substance abuse or anger at a church policy, the laws of emotional triangles remind you that the more you try to change the other relationship, the more entrenched it will become.

So, in many, if not most, cases, working with the symptomatic will not help the situation and will often make it worse. If a counselor works solely with the symptomatic member, things are not likely to improve. Because the focus is on the person with the symptoms, it has the effect of absolving others of responsibility and making it even less likely that the system will seek positive change. There may be sessions with other family members, but the attention is squarely on "the one with the problem." In fact, this process often makes the symptomatic one feel even more helpless and unmotivated to change.

Understanding family systems theory and the nature of relationship systems helps you to understand that modifying the input of ANY person in the system can be a catalyst for change. Of course, this starts with you. If you are a member of the system, examine yourself. How has your input in the past contributed to the symptom? Were you reactive? Adaptive? How can you respond as a non-anxious presence? If your own input into the system is a problem, then start with that.

However, if you are a leader, you can also view the entire system and look at ways to help it change in positive, life-giving ways. This is hard work and can be painful, but it's the only way forward. This is the basis for the coaching approach. This typically works with a non-symptomatic member of the system. The focus is to change input into the system by someone who has more capacity to bring change.

There are two criteria for identifying who has the greatest capacity to bring change to the system. First, the person must have an emotional connection with the symptomatic person. Recall from Chapter 8 that chronic conditions can only become chronic if there is reactive or adaptive feedback from other members connected to the identified patient (symptomatic person). If a person has an emotional connection with the symptomatic one, then they are likely providing some kind of feedback that contributes to the problem and/or helps it to persist. This means that the potential is to change that feedback through self-differentiation. This will cause the system to react and gives it the opportunity to seek positive change. Of course, it also means there will be sabotage and things will get worse before they get better (see Chapter 8).

Which leads to the second criterion for identifying who has the greatest capacity to bring change to the system: motivation. In my experience, the motivated person is so tired of the way things are, the current homeostasis, that they are willing to endure a tremendous amount of pain to make things better. This pain includes examining themselves, doing their own work, as well as enduring the pain that comes from the inevitable sabotage that comes from the change in their behavior. Over the years I have worked with people who sought change in both families of origin and church systems. They all start out saying they want things to change. Very few have the motivation and resolve to stay the course when the sabotage comes. The motivated ones initiated real change, lasting improvement and helped to move the system to a new, healthier homeostasis.

What the coaching model does is to start by helping this motivated person to examine her own anxiety. The coach challenges her to find the unresolved issues in her own family of origin to get to what is driving her reactivity to the current situation. The coach then encourages her to rework the unresolved relationship. This can take time, be painful and may require a therapist. The coach can also help her to anticipate the patterns in the current situation and practice non-anxious responses through role-play. The more playful and paradoxical the responses, the better. In most cases, the person being coached can predict how things will go down with the symptomatic one. By role-playing responses, she is better able to self-differentiate when it matters most. These responses move from the initial non-reactive responses to being a non-anxious presence through the sabotage. This is the hardest part. It doesn't always work, because if there is a failure of nerve, the old reactive responses come back. Unless she can correct herself in future responses, the system will have succeeded in pushing her back into the old homeostasis.

As a leader, you are often the one who meets the two criteria for being coached in the congregational system. You are connected to the most people in the church, including the symptomatic one. You are also motivated to seek positive change. Even if you don't meet the two criteria, your responsibility as a leader is to be aware enough of how the system is functioning to try to identify how change might occur. At the very least, this means finding those most motivated to change and then finding them the resources to do it. More likely, it means leading through self-differentiation in the triangles to which you belong.

The Power of Staying in Triangles

You may have been advised by a well-meaning mentor or advisor to stay out of triangles. This means avoiding getting triangled if possible, and getting out of them quickly, if needed. While this makes sense and will save you some stress and aggravation, it diminishes your power as a leader. Why? Because you can't change a relationship to which you don't belong. While this means you can never change the relationship of the other two legs of the triangle, getting out of the triangle also lessens the opportunity to change the relationship between you and each of the two legs. Remember that any input into the system can change the overall functioning of the system. So, if you change the way you relate to one of the two legs of a triangle -- that is, change your input or feedback -- without disconnecting emotionally, it will increase the pressure on her to change. Homeostatic forces will cause her to push back through sabotage, but if you can maintain your non-anxious presence, then change is possible. This can have the cascading effect of changing the relationship of the other two members.

Just as so many aspects of the family systems approach are counterintuitive, staying in triangles sounds like a bad idea. And it can be if you don't function in healthy ways. If you focus on trying to change the other two or if you can't help but be reactive, then you are part of the problem, not the solution. However, if you are doing your own work and learning to lead through self-differentiation, then it is worth considering the value of staying in the triangle. Friedman puts it this way: "Staying in a triangle without getting triangled oneself gives one far more power than never entering the triangle in the first place. Many slick and charming leaders never get stressed because they intuitively stay out of triangles; but that makes them less effective."[3]

There is a difference between de-triangling and disconnecting. The former does not mean you get out of the triangle. It does not mean you disconnect emotionally with either or both of the two sides. It DOES mean that you remain a non-anxious presence. You give back the responsibility for their relationship while staying connected. This is different than disconnecting.

How do you make others responsible? Well, you can't MAKE them responsible, but you can refuse to take responsibility. You can increase your own threshold to their pain. You can remain connected without overfunctioning. Put simply, you can lead through self-differentiation.

Everything discussed thus far leads to this: You have the power to lead change. The more anxious the system, whether family, church or organization, the harder it will be and the longer it will take. But I have seen this happen over and over again. I have seen leaders who get right to the brink of a breakthrough, have a failure of nerve, and then things never change. I have seen others who persist, managing their own anxiety and feedback, which ultimately breaks the entire system free from its old patterns. The choice is yours. It's all you have.

Chapter 11
Doing Your Own Work

So now you know what it means to lead through self-differentiation. The good news is that many have gone this way before. With God's help, YOU can do it. But YOU have to do it. Nobody else can do it for you (and you should wary of those who try).

What to Expect

According to Jenny Brown from the Family Systems Institute, there are three stages in working toward self-differentiation.[1]

These are:

Stage 1: Reduce anxiety by learning how symptomatic behavior, either that of yourself or others, is part of relationship patterns in the system. This can be both in the congregational system and in the family of origin. It is working through anxiety in the latter that will enable better functioning in all relationships.

Stage 2: Focus on the ability to self-define to increase self-differentiation, while resisting the pull of surrounding togetherness pressures. You articulate your own goals and values and identify the surrounding togetherness pressures that make it difficult to self-define. You do this in a safe place without actually trying to change how you relate in the system.

Stage 3: Learn how to function in self-differentiated ways. This is a coaching process where you anticipate situations in your family of origin that increase anxiety and then practice how you can function as a non-anxious presence. This will increase your ability to self-differentiate in all situations, including your nuclear family and the congregational system. It's important to remember that self-differentiation includes both self-definition and emotional connection. During this stage you learn to take emotional stands while staying connected to those who make you most anxious.

Brown writes, "The goal of therapy is to assist family members towards greater levels of differentiation, where there is less blaming, decreased reactivity and increased responsibility for self in the emotional system."[2] This is done by identifying the relationships in your family of origin that cause the most anxiety, unearthing what makes them anxiety producing, then reworking how you function in those relationships to better self-differentiate. It is not easy work. It is likely to be painful. The thought of taking emotional stands in your most challenging relationships will scare you. The choice is yours. You can do something about your anxiety, or you can leave things alone.

You've come this far. You might as well get started. So, let's look at the tools that you'll use to do your own work.

The Genogram

The genogram is both your foundation and your road map. It gives you a way to organize all your thoughts and to learn about your family of origin. It also points you in the right direction to understand which relationships have unresolved issues.

A genogram is a family tree. It is diagrammed in the same way. Each generation is on its own horizontal level. Older generations are higher, and younger generations are lower.

There are also lines or markings to indicate emotional distance such as appropriate closeness, fusion (too close), cut-off (too distant) and conflict. There are shadings to indicate physical or psychological illness. There are markings to represent marital status, as well as childbearing events such as adoption, miscarriage and abortion.

The point here is not to teach you how to do a genogram. It's to help you understand how this graphic representation can help you understand the emotional patterns in your family of origin. Much of what you discover will seem obvious. But it's likely that you have been ignoring or even denying its existence. This will be especially true if you have trouble managing anxiety.

Your genogram will help you identify where you have unresolved issues in your family of origin. Let's face it. We all have issues. Nobody gets the problem they can handle. This truly is the beginning of doing your own work. Once you identify the source(s) of your anxiety, you can then begin the work of changing how you function. It's hard work, but it's worth it.

The Family Timeline

Like the genogram, the family timeline is another tool that will help you to understand your family of origin. The purpose is to lay out the arc of your family history, as well as the significant events that help define your family. You should do a separate timeline for both the maternal and paternal sides of your family. And, depending on how long you have been an adult, you may want to do another timeline that starts with you and includes your own significant events, relationships and offspring, if any.

The overall arc includes emigrations, relocations, employment changes, births, deaths, marriages, divorces, military service, etc. You can also provide world or regional events that help provide context. For example, the Japanese invasion of Pearl Harbor in 1941 changed everything for both sides of my family. My mother and siblings were living with their aunt in Japan while her parents ran the family business in Seattle. War between the U.S. and Japan created the uncertainty that the family may never be reunited. I know they ultimately were reunited, but the uncertainty itself can be identified as a source of anxiety in the system. Likewise, as mentioned in Chapter 1, my father's family was interned in Idaho. Pearl Harbor was the defining moment that started this process.

Your timeline will be most useful if you include other significant, family defining events. Examples include: arrests and imprisonments; betrayals; business formations or breakups; prolonged battles with disease; and the origins of ongoing disputes. Your family timeline can include anything that you or another family member recalls quickly as something that has shaped who you are. It will take some time to do, but it is worth the effort, because it will help you to decipher the code that defines your family.

The Importance of Stories

The genogram and family timeline will require you to speak to family members. More importantly, it will require you to listen to their stories. This may be intimidating, but there's no way around it. This is how you will crack the code to your family of origin.

The most daunting part will be engaging with those who make you most anxious. This is especially true if that person is a parent. The best way to approach this is to start somewhere else. If you have living grandparents, they are a great source of stories. Not only will you hear stories that help you understand the family, you will also hear stories about your parents from an entirely different perspective. Aunts and uncles are another great source. It's likely that you and they will feel much lower emotional stakes. Because they aren't your parents, they may share things that they wouldn't with their own children. They can provide perspective on your parents and grandparents that illuminate your understanding of your family's functioning.

Anxiety is transmitted from generation to generation. Most times it's done unknowingly. Molly S. Castelloe, Ph.D., cites the work of M. Gerard Fromm in her *Psychology Today* article, "How Trauma Is Carried Across Generations: Holding the secret history of our ancestors." She writes:

"The transmission of trauma may be particular to a given family suffering a loss, such as the death of an infant, or it can be a shared response to societal trauma. Maurice De Witt, a sidewalk Santa on Fifth Avenue noticed a marked change in behavior the holiday season following 9/11 when parents would not 'let the hands of their children go. The kids sense that. It's like water seeping down, and the kids can feel it... There is an anxiety, but the kids can't make the connections.' 'This astute man was noticing a powerful double message in the parent's action,' Fromm says. 'Consciously and verbally, the message was "Here's Santa. Love him." Unconsciously and physically, it was "Here's Santa. Fear him." The unnamed trauma of 9/11 was communicated to the next generation by the squeeze of a hand.' Psychic legacies are often passed on through unconscious cues or affective messages that flow between child and adult. Sometimes anxiety falls from one generation to the next through stories told."[3]

It's hard to overestimate the importance of releasing the anxiety of unresolved issues. Sometimes we don't even know that the anxiety exists.

My mother was born in Seattle in 1923. Her father and his brothers owned a wholesale seafood business. They were the first non-Anglo business on the Seattle waterfront. But my grandfather sent the family back to Japan in 1933 to help the business survive the Great Depression. Her mother came back to Seattle a few years later to be with her husband. My mom and her four siblings stayed with their aunt in Hiroshima until 1947. I grew up hearing my mother's stories of life in Japan. Most of them centered around what life was like being separated from her parents while her own country, the U.S., and her country of origin and residence, Japan, were at war. Some of them were about the A-bomb. Her family was fortunate. Of the five children, only the youngest, Nobu, was killed in the blast. She was 15. I don't know if the stories transmitted anxiety or not. I do know that I'm glad they were told.

Six years ago my Aunt called me on my birthday. She doesn't usually call. When she did, she said, "Happy Birthday! Same birthday as Nobu."

I wanted to say, "What?! I have the same birthday as my aunt who was killed by the A-bomb, and nobody told me?" I thanked my aunt for telling me and told her that I had never known this, using the best non-anxious response I could muster. Then I called my mom and asked her about it.

"What? Hmmm. Oh yeah, I guess you do have the same birthday. I guess I forgot about it."

I wonder what anxiety was transmitted by not telling me? I wonder what anxiety was released when I found out? I can't really answer it, but it felt like a good thing to find out. It binds me in a special way to my family heritage that I can't explain.

As my own experience demonstrates, you won't always understand everything you learn. You won't be able to assign value to all that you hear. Listening to your family's stories is just the beginning. You then need a way to process it.

You Can't Do This Alone

Doing your own work requires you to go more deeply into your relationships in order to unpack and decode the unwritten rules of your family system. You can do a lot of thinking about this, but it's impossible without help. Fortunately, you have options.

The best option is to find a family systems therapist. Family systems theory was developed by Murray Bowen, so you want to find someone who specializes in family systems therapy or "Bowenian family therapy." This doesn't mean you need to bring your whole family into sessions with your therapist. It means she will help you to view your situation from a systems perspective and will help you to work through the stages of the self-differentiation process. If your family of origin is characterized by one or more of the following situations, it may be impossible to do your own work without a professional therapist:

- Constant, debilitating anxiety and conflict

- Emotional cut-offs -- meaning people do not speak to each other for months or years at a time due to unresolved conflict

- Intense trauma such as abuse, violence or forced separations

Anyone can benefit from a therapist, but the greater the unresolved issues, the more necessary a therapist becomes.

Another option is to find a coach who uses a family systems approach. This is not a professional therapist, but someone who has done their own work and understands how to walk you through the process. Coaching can be done one-on-one or in a group setting. The coach will help you to use the tools already described so you can work your way through the stages of the self-differentiation process. You may want to work with a coach for a limited period of time, perhaps six months to a year. Or, like a therapist, you may feel the coach can help you over the long-term to modify your input into the systems to which you belong, both as a family member and as a leader.

Finally, you can find a program that specifically focuses on the family systems approach to congregational leadership. I list several of these in the resource section of this book. These are comprised of a series of multi-day workshops or retreats where you will do your own work, all within the context of serving in the church. You will be with the same cohort of persons throughout the process, which makes the process a combination of group learning and group coaching.

You may find that you use more than one of these approaches. This is a life's work. If the best we can hope for is 70% self-differentiation, then there is always room to improve. But the benefits are priceless. You will be a better family member, a better person and a better leader.

It's Your Move

What happens next is up to you. You can set this book down and get on with your life. Or you can start (or continue) your journey toward greater self-differentiation. You can try to lead change, only to retreat when the sabotage gets too intense. Or you can find yourself and, in the process, discover how you can sustain a non-anxious presence in the midst of anxiety and resistance. If you are willing to make the effort, you can expect to be able to:

- Articulate your values, beliefs and vision, while giving others the freedom to disagree, even in the midst of surrounding togetherness pressures

- Better recognize emotional triangles

- Work to remain a non-anxious presence in the triangles to which you belong

- Better manage stress

- Better regulate your own anxiety and your input into the systems to which you belong

- Stop trying to convince others to agree with you, and believe in what God is leading you to do

- Discern the difference between those who are trying to help you and those who are trying to change you

The list goes on. By now you get it. I believe God is calling leaders who get it. And your willingness to do what is necessary to lead through self-differentiation could make the difference in your church. It could mean the difference between a church that thrives and one that merely survives, or even dies. The question is what will you do next?

It's your move.

Appendix

If you haven't accessed the FREE Companion Course for this book, you can do so at www.christian-leaders.com/anxious-book-course.

It may be time for you to read or re-read Edwin Friedman's books. I've mentioned two of the three already.

Generation to Generation: Family Process in Church and Synagogue

The seminal work that applies Murray Bowen's family systems theory to congregational leadership. It is difficult material, but after reading my book, it may be easier to understand. It has been my constant companion throughout my ministry.

Friedman's Fables

Just as Jesus told parables to illustrate concepts of God's reign, Friedman uses fables to help us understand family systems. You could actually use this book without Generation to Generation, but it's best to use them together.

A Failure of Nerve: Leadership in the Age of the Quick Fix

Friedman was working on this book when he died in 1996. It was completed by family and colleagues. It was published ten years after his death. It takes Generation to Generation a step further and applies it to the larger society with amazing insight.

Programs to Do Your Own Work

The following programs can help you do your own work without a therapist. This is a personal decision. Many people are able to do this. Some are not. If you try this approach, you can always decide to see a therapist if you realize you need more help.

I've listed programs that can help you work through your own functioning in your family of origin. They are designed for leaders in the congregational context. I know those who lead the program and/or have heard positive feedback from people who have participated. There are certainly others, but I can only recommend those that I know.

I've listed the Center for Family Process first, since this was founded by Edwin Friedman.

Center for Family Process
Bethesda, MD
http://www.centerforfamilyprocess.com/

Center for Clergy Excellence
Centreville, MD
http://www.pecometh.org/clergy-excellence

Center for Pastoral Effectiveness of the Rockies
Highlands Ranch, CO
http://www.pastoraleffectiveness.org/

Lombard Mennonite Peace Center
Lombard, IL
https://www.lmpeacecenter.org/workshops/lac/

Tending the Fire
Northeastern U.S.
http://tending-the-fire.com/

Acknowledgments

It's been a dream to write and publish a book. I couldn't have done it without the help of family, friends and colleagues. My wife, Jodi, has supported this project from day one, as well as helped proofread early editions. In addition, I worked with some great professionals. Lee Constantine from Publishizer guided my crowdfunding campaign. The following made this a book that I'm proud of: Kendall Davis, Developmental Editor; Colby Hochmuth, Copy Editor; Trinity McFadden, Proofreader; and Claire Purnell, Graphic Designer.

Thank you to all of those who showed faith in me by supporting the publication of this book financially. The following SPONSORS provided major support:

- Steve Wilke and The Institute for Discipleship-BeADisciple.com
- Rev. Tom Pasmore and Avenue United Methodist Church, Milford, Delaware
- D.R. Barton Jr.
- Jennings and Lisa Hastings
- Roy Kirby Jr.
- Rev. Karen Handy and St. Luke's United Methodist Church, Denton, Maryland

My cousin, Alan Kurimura, supported this book in memory of our grandmother, Sada "Mama" Shitama. Like so many strong women, Mama raised our parents as a single mother. She was a true leader and teacher of her five children.

Finally, thank you to each of the following, who bought one or more copies of the book before it was even finished. You made its publication possible:

Charlotte Abel
Charles Adams
Georgieanna
   Anderson
Carolyn Aoki
Joseph Archie
Jonathan Baker
Ken Banaszak
John Barteld
Cathie Barton
Bernadette
   Beckett
David Berkey
Carol Biggs
Richard Browne
Mary Browne
David Buchanan
John Bunts
Herb Cain
Joseph Cain
Bill Carroll
Dan Carwile
Drew Christian
Lois Coder
Frank Coleman
Rebecca Collison
Jeffrey Connors

Sharon Cook
Will Cooper
Alan Coppage
Carl Davis
Leslie Diestel
Kerry Dietz
Miles Dissinger
Karen Dize
Tom Duffy
Fred Duncan
Debra Ebling
Ray Eck
Helene Elzey
Carmella Evans
Gary Fellows
Rita Fry
Janis Gatzke
Kent Gladish
Don Goehner
Morris Gold
Richard
   Goldman
Vicki
   Gordy-Stith
Neil Gutmaker
Mari Hammon
Lu Harding

Sara Harrison
Marian Harvey
Constance
   Hastings
Jeffrey Hayes
Dolores Hazel
Misa Heater
Bruce Hemphill
Franklin W.
   Hendricks
Tom Hershey
David Hill
Dickie Hinton
Lisa Jean
   Hoefner
Cat Holbert
Thea Horii
John Hornberger
Barry Hudson
David Humphrey
John Jackson
Preston Jacquette
Yumi Jarris
Emanuel Johnson
Kari Jones
Naomi Joy
Amy Julian
Scott Kane

Thomas Kearns
David Kelley
Thomas Kihara
Cindy Koski
Alan Kurimura
Augie Lankford
Gary Lawson Sr.
Julie Lewis
Beverly Lewis
Barbara Lort
Jen Mabry
Sharon Mankin
Hana Jane
    Maroon
Elizabeth
    Marrero
Lynn McCord
George
    McKeown
Karen
    McLachlan
David McMillan
Stanley Menking
Jason Middleton
Apryl Miller
Shane Moran
Karen Morgan
Donald
    Mulholland
Jeanie Nelson
Jody Oates
Bruce Obenshain
Brent O'Neill

Ren Orans
Paul Owens
Carlton Parker
Larry Peacock
Lawrence Pelham
Derrick Porter
Brad Powers
Gary Priddy
Carol Psaros
Claire Purnell
Regina Reeves
Missy Rekitzke
Carlos Reyes
Delila Robinson
    Parham
Bruce Rogers
James Ruark
Pat Saito
Ronald Schatz
Bradley Schutt
David Segermark
Carol Shaw
Sally Sheldon
Ben Shitama
Erin Shitama
Hoch Shitama
Noah Shitama
Zach Shitama
Tayeko Shitama
Bonnie Shively
Thomas Short
Dean Snyder
Carolyn Spencer

Joyce Stansfield
Kelli Stansfield
Jeanel Starling
Brian Stepnitz
Sally Stewart
Richard Stoltzfus
Lauri & Jay Stout
Nelson Stubbs
Janet Thomas
Mary Jane Titter
Rob Townsend
Asher Tunik
Jon Uota
Aimee Urata
Richard Vance
Eileen Viars
Cindy Wallace
Eric Warner
Loretta
    Washburn
Roslyn Watts
Bill Webb
Charles Weber
Tina Whaley
Julie Whitmore
Cary & Hilda
    Williams
Kevin Witt
Diane Wood
Bernadette
    Wright
Amy & Ray
    Yarnall
Barbara Zasowski

About the Author

Jack Shitama has been leading change in ministry settings since 1991. He has led growth in small churches. He guided the transformation of a professional association. He proposed and executed a plan for the sale and replacement of a beloved denominational institution. Jack is an ordained United Methodist minister and the founding Minister-in-Residence of the Center for Clergy Excellence in Centreville, MD. Jack and his wife, Jodi, have four adult children and one grandchild. They live with no kids and no pets on Maryland's Eastern Shore.

Learn more at www.christian-leaders.com.

Contact him at jack@christian-leaders.com.

Notes

Chapter 1

1. Seth Godin, *The opposite of anxiety*, Seth's Blog, August 2, 2013, http://sethgodin.typepad.com/seths_blog/2013/08/the-opposite-of-anxiety.html .

2. Edwin H. Friedman, *Generation to Generation: Family Process in Church and Synagogue* (New York: The Guildford Press, 1985), 27.

3. Goodreads, *Martin Luther King, Jr.* > Quotes, https://www.goodreads.com/author/quotes/23924.Martin_Luther_King_Jr_.

Chapter 2

1. Friedman, 229.

Chapter 3

1. Friedman, 28-29.

2. Friedman, 53.

Chapter 4

1. Edwin H. Friedman, *A Failure of Nerve: Leadership in the Age of the Quick Fix* (New York: Seabury Books, 1999, 2007), 59-60.

2. John A. Johnson, Ph.D., "Are 'I' Statements Better than 'You' Statements?," Psychology Today, November 30, 2012, https://www.psychologytoday.com/blog/cui-bono/201211/are-i-statements-better-you-statements.

3. https://www.psychologytoday.com/blog/cui-bono/201211/are-i-statements-better-you-statements.

4. https://www.psychologytoday.com/blog/cui-bono/201211/are-i-statements-better-you-statements.

5. Merriam-Webster.com, "Homeostasis," https://www.merriam-webster.com/dictionary/homeostasis.

Chapter 5

1. Stephen R. Covey, *The 7 Habits of Highly Effective People*, "Habit 2: Begin with the End in Mind," Stephen R. Covey, https://www.stephencovey.com/7habits/7habits-habit2.php.

2. Simon Sinek, "How great leaders inspire action," https://www.ted.com/talks/simon_sinek_how_great_leaders_inspire_action.

3. Friedman, *Generation to Generation*, 30.

Chapter 6

1. Dictionary.com, "Distress," http://www.dictionary.com/browse/distress.

2. Merriam-Webster.com, "Eustress," https://www.merriam-webster.com/dictionary/eustress.

3. Viktor E. Frankl, *Man's Search for Meaning* (Boston: Beacon Press, 2006), 112.

4. Frankl, 86.

5. Friedman, *A Failure of Nerve*, 220.

Chapter 8

1. Leander S. Harding, "Misreading Family Systems Theory," leanderharding.com, https://leanderharding.com/2008/05/28/misreading-family-systems-theory/.

2. https://leanderharding.com/2008/05/28/misreading-family-systems-theory/.

3. Stephen R. Covey, Roger A. Merrill, Rebecca R. Merrill, *First Things First* (New York: Simon & Schuster, 1994), 167.

Chapter 9

1. Brené Brown, "The Power of Vulnerability," https://www.ted.com/talks/brene_brown_on_vulnerability.

2. Brené Brown, *Daring Greatly: How the Courage to Be Vulnerable Transforms the Way We Live* (New York: Gotham Books, 2012), 37.

3. Brown, 2.

4. Seth Godin, *Out on a Limb*, Seth's Blog, January 5, 2013, http://sethgodin.typepad.com/seths_blog/2013/01/out-on-a-limb.html.

5. http://sethgodin.typepad.com/seths_blog/2013/01/out-on-a-limb.html.

6. https://www.ted.com/talks/brene_brown_on_vulnerability.

Chapter 10

1. Friedman, *Generation to Generation*, 225.

2. Friedman, *Generation to Generation*, 226.

3. Friedman, A Failure of Nerve, 234.

Chapter 11

1. Jenny Brown, "Bowen Family Systems Theory and Practice: Illustration and Critique," The Family Systems Institute, http://www.thefsi.com.au/wp-content/uploads/2014/01/Bowen-Family-Systems-Theory-and-Practice_Illustration-and-Critique.pdf, 6.

2. http://www.thefsi.com.au/wp-content/uploads/2014/b01/Bowen-Family-Systems-Theory-and-Practice_Illustration-and-Critique.pdf, 6.

3. Molly S. Castelloe, Ph.D., "How Trauma Is Carried Across Generations: Holding the secret history of our ancestors," https://www.psychologytoday.com/blog/the-me-in-we/201205/how-trauma-is-carried-across-generations.